Are parents always more ambitious for their children than they are for themselves? (Jeffrey Archer)

CONTENTS

    Introduction

1   Increasing Potential   1

2   High Expectations   10

3   Goals   14

4   Learning Skills   20

    Distributing Practice Time   21

    Repetition   23

    Sleep Learning   33

    Chunking   36

5   The Time Thief   39

6   The Metaskills of Achievement   46

    Motivation   46

    Autonomy   51

    Praise   53

    Relationships   60

    Competence   61

    Flow   62

    Enjoyment   66

    Self-Discipline   67

    Attitude and Perseverance   69

7   Metacognition   72

	Questioning	75
	Self-Talk	78
	Reflection	79
8	IQ and Intelligence	81
	Multiple Intelligence	84
9	Creativity	88
	Bibliography	95
	About The Author	97

INTRODUCTION

To fully address issues pertaining to children and learning would require a book of epic magnitude. The purpose of this book is not to be comprehensive, but rather, to concentrate on a few select fundamentals for reaching success. Essentially, this entails a *can-do* mindset, an understanding of the mechanics of how learning occurs - and the time it takes, and the development of character traits such as commitment and perseverance.

Parents are disadvantaged in that they are mostly unaware of the teaching expertise of those in charge of their children's education. Not all good teaching and learning is intuitive, and so I address assumptions behind systemic teaching interventions such as praise and building self-esteem, from an evidence perspective.

The book is written with the general reader in mind. I have tried to keep jargon to a minimum, and have provided the references most useful as footnotes, as well as a bibliography for further reading.

CHILDREN AND LEARNING – FOR PARENTS

1   INCREASING POTENTIAL

Why is it that some people achieve so much more than others? This, is a crucial, over-arching question for every parent and educator. Essentially, people respond to this in one of two ways. Camp A believe that learning achievement is pre-determined by a genetic endowment; a natural gift, or talent. Camp B attribute success from environmental and character factors. Most people take an each way bet. They think achievement requires hard work, opportunities, parental encouragement and so forth, but is not possible without the X factor, a genetic talent essential for reaching excellence. Rather than belonging to a new Camp C though, this viewpoint still lives in Camp A, as the genetic requirement is paramount. Teacher/parent attribution of a child's potential is the foundation for future success or failure. It cannot be over-emphasized how important this is.

Logically, knowledge and ability can only come from genetic endowment or living experience, so it must be one or the other, or the each way bet theory. However, an ever-growing body of research confirms that parents and teachers in Camp B foster in their children a mindset that believes in the transformative power of the quality and quantity of effort, resulting in greater achievement. In a sense, it does not even matter what the truth of the answer to the genetic question is, because belief in one's capacity to improve accompanied by quality and quantity of work is a recipe for success. Nevertheless, what is the evidence for Camp A's intellectual gene argument?

The Human Genome Project was the world's largest

international biological project. Prior to the project, the assumption was that variant genes that determined human abilities and characteristics would be discovered, and that human complexity and variability would necessitate a genome consisting of more than 100,000 genes. From 1990 till 2003 the HGP worked to identify and map the genome. The result? It found that humans have 99.9 percent identical genetic structure among just 22,300 genes. The project was stunningly unsuccessful in that it did not find variant genes associated with intelligence, exceptional performance, or special ability.[1] Long-held assumptions about genetic determinism have not been supported by evidence.

> Except for height, there is no firm empirical evidence for innate talent influencing expert performance. The real key to understanding expert and exceptional performance is in the motivational factors that lead a small number of individuals to maintain the effortful pursuit of their best performance during their productive career, when most other individuals have settled for a merely acceptable level. (K Anders Ericsson)[2]

According to talent theory, lucky individuals win the genetic lottery. They are born with learning talents and fortunate circumstances allow these to be nurtured. The problem with this theory is that for many skills and abilities, specific genes associated

---

[1] James, O. 2016. Not in your Genes. London. Vermillion
[2] Ericsson, K. A. 2016. Peak: Secrets from the New Science of Expertise. Boston, MA: Houghton Mifflin Harcourt.

with these have not been found. Take music for example. Despite the lack of genetic evidence, musical ability is more often considered genetically derived than any other ability or human faculty. Evidence for this is anecdotal and stories of exceptional prodigies abound. How, for example, could Mozart's precocity be explained in any other way?

Mozart's feats can be explained rationally. Like all great composers, his biography reveals substantial and sustained early training, supported by family and tutors. It is difficult to separate fact from fiction 230 years after the event, but we do know that Mozart was immersed in a concentrated musical environment from his earliest days. His father, Leopold, was an excellent music educator. He wrote the first ever book on musical training for children. Leopold devoted his life to teach his son, working with him full time from the age of four, and took every opportunity to promote Wolfgang's musical ability. Camille Saint-Saens said, "History is made up of what probably happened; mythology of what probably did not happen. There are myths in history and history in myths". Stories such as that of two-year-old Wolfgang identifying the sound of pig squeals as G-sharp should be taken with a grain of salt, as they were most likely spawned by his father, who was not always honest about his children's musical abilities. Leopold was known to subtract a year from the ages of Wolfgang and Nannerl, when advertising their performances. Leopold was a smart operator. He knew that lowering his children's ages would augment their specialness. There is nothing unusual about parents embellishing facts to help their children get noticed. Mozart's childhood compositions indicate assistance from his father, as well as themes borrowed from Johann Christian Bach, with whom Mozart collaborated in London at the age of nine. Imitation is a healthy and natural part of the learning process, and lying about a child's age does not detract from the evident skill. But it does skew the picture. The possibility that Mozart's great desire to make music was rooted in pre-birth fortune cannot be ruled out, but his early musical environment was encouraging and inspiring. Having a great passion for music—and a supportive if demanding, micro-managing and opportunistic father—led him to take advantage of his opportunities and to practise for several hours a day from the age of two. In Genius Explained, Michael Howe estimates that Mozart accrued about 3,500 hours of practice by age six, reaching an accumulated practice figure of 10,000 hours by the age of eight.[3]

Even if you cling to the position that a child is born with genetic potential, the assumed natural talent that differentiates children becomes less evident as they age, as dedication and sheer hard work play greater roles in achievement. Malcolm Gladwell says, "The further a career develops, the less important the role of assumed innate ability in comparison with preparation or practice".[4] Quality and quantity of practice develops expertise.

> She plays so well because she has a talent. How do I know she has a talent? That's obvious, she plays so well! (Michael Howe)

---

[3] Howe, M. J. 1999. Genius Explained. Cambridge: Cambridge University Press.
[4] Gladwell, M. 2008. Outliers. London: Penguin.

In every case, talent is identified retrospectively, and the emergence of prodigious skill follows rather than precedes unique opportunity and substantial work. Investigations of superior achievement suggest that precocity is the result of early childhood experiences, parental support, a young starting age, training, practice hours, habits, metacognitive skills and opportunity. What distinguishes prodigies is that they are constantly compared with children their own age, rather than with others who have accrued a similar number of practice hours, and similar opportunities and family support.

Stanford University professor Carol Dweck warns that students who are praised for innate talent rather than effort are at risk of developmental problems. In her book Mindset: The New Psychology of Success, Dweck presents a strong case that a focus on genetic gifts can lead to a poor work ethic. Children with this fixed intelligence mindset get the impression that because they have natural ability they do not need to work as hard as normal children. People identified as naturally talented or gifted can be protective of their special labels and tend to avoid challenges or risks that might lead to failure. Appearing smart and proving their intelligence, at the expense of improving it, must be preserved at all costs. This mindset is more likely to lead to hiding rather than correcting mistakes, and following a setback these individuals are less persistent than growth mindset individuals. Hence the typical combination emerges: gifted and lazy. If one does not try very hard and fails, one keeps the "special" tag. "If I try my best and still fail – disaster!" On the other hand, people who believe their intelligence is a potential to be developed through effort are less worried about short-term mistakes, difficulties, and failures. They accept these events as an essential part of the learning process. People with this growth intelligence mindset tend to reach higher levels of achievement and enjoy the learning challenges inherent in the process. The advantage of the growth intelligence mindset is that one does not just learn how to succeed but also how to persevere when one fails. Growth intelligence mindset children are more likely to embrace the challenges and difficulties that lead to mastery. We don't improve in anything without pushing beyond our comfort zone. To prove or improve my intelligence; that is the mindset question.

Given the lack of evidence for genetic talent, and the evidence of a range of mindset and learning issues for those who attribute their achievement to it, one wonders why people so desperately want to maintain an allegiance to talent theory. An external attribution of immutable talent creates an excuse for failing, reducing the responsibility of parents, teachers and students. It can be used to excuse lack of effort, and for quitting. Parents claim, "He tried it, but gave it away because he just isn't mathematical" (we could tell because he found it difficult).

It is not easy to teach learning strategies to fixed-intelligence-mindset students who have deep-set beliefs about their potential. Unless this mindset is reformed, they emerge as adults with stifling doubts about their capacity to learn. Kenny Werner refers to "the menacing voices from childhood".[5] The struggle to learn is very often a result of being told that the task is really difficult, or you have not the talent for it. The word difficult can be discouraging. I like Werner's suggestion to explain task complexity in terms of unfamiliar and familiar rather than difficult and easy. By attributing failure to lack of effort or poor learning strategies, rather than natural ability, teachers and parents can help transform mindset.

Confidence is central in positive psychology. It centres on self-belief in one's ability to achieve goals. Confidence that results from progress through effort has enormous worth. The level of confidence prior to a performance examination is a predictor of the examination result. When taking music examinations, for example, students with a high level of confidence outperform their peers with similar skills but lower expectations. Robert Sternberg says, "The best predictor of success among students is in their belief in their ability to succeed".[6] Top-performing athletes spend a great deal of time cultivating an indomitable spirit of self-belief. Perhaps no other sportsperson exemplified this to the degree of heavyweight boxer and Athlete of the Century Muhammad Ali. Prior to a bout, Ali stood before the media proclaiming, "I am the greatest". Some viewed his actions as egotistical, even comical, but the power that accompanied Ali's confidence was extraordinary. Action follows feeling. This principle was proposed by the father of psychology William James, who said it also works the other way: if you deliberately act, feelings follow.

---

[5] Werner, Kenny. 1996. Effortless Mastery. New Albany, IN: Jamey Aebersold.
[6] Sternberg, R. J. and Grigorenko, E. L. 2000. Teaching for Successful Intelligence to Increase Student Learning and Achievement. Arlington Heights, IL: Skylight.

Action and feelings go together. Muhammad Ali's self-belief was essential for his performance, and his repeated self-affirmations nurtured it to an extraordinary level.

> It is the repetition of affirmations that leads to belief. Once that belief becomes a deep conviction, things begin to happen. (Muhammad Ali)

The notion of talent prevails in the world of sport. In the 2010 Football World Cup, titleholder Italy was supremely confident of their ability to defeat the semi-professional New Zealand team, so much so that pre-match media comments suggested arrogance and contempt for the skill level of their opponents. Given that on the world market one Italian player was worth three times the value of the New Zealand team, Italy's attitude was perhaps understandable. However, Italy failed to defeat New Zealand and was bundled out of the World Cup. Italy's problem was a focus on natural ability. The New Zealand team focussed on work ethic. Passion, the first step in achievement, can outperform talent.

A fixed intelligence mindset stifles progress, leading to underachievement, less effort, and ineffective learning strategies. It acts as a barrier to further attempts, inducing learned helplessness. The students who end up being brilliant and expert are those who work the hardest and the smartest. This is the level playing field.

When people don't know how to do something that others can, the gap can seem so unreachable, they may not even try. "How does he move his fingers so fast? I could never do that!" This is the reason

Chinese pianist and music world phenomenon Lang Lang gave for writing his autobiography: "because nobody really knows how we musicians got to where we are. All my colleagues in classical music have worked this hard, but nobody knows just how hard".[7] The casual observer sees the performance like they do an iceberg, blind to the 90 percent of practice activity that lies beneath the surface. Virtuosity is attainable if you don't mind working. began learning piano before the age of three and was practising about six hours per day at age five. This soon increased to 8–10 hours per day and, despite being fired by his teacher at age nine for having no talent, he prevailed. Lang Lang is a champion of the growth mindset. He credits his consistently rigorous practice for his success.

> I believe you have all the talent and creativity you need. What you can control is how hard you work. You can make sure you work harder than anyone else. (Lang Lang)

---

[7] Lang L. 2008. Journey of a Thousand Miles. New York: Spiegel & Grau.

2   HIGH EXPECTATIONS

Imagine a school system that incorporated a structure where all children were asked to commit to seeking expertise in an area of their choice, as a special project alongside the traditional comprehensive education. Students would gain a deeper understanding of the requirements to reach for the top. They would practise the all-important metacognitive strategies of goal setting, monitoring, self-evaluation and reflection, discussed later in this book. They would realise that quality and quantity of effort is the achievement game changer. The act of commitment, perseverance and resolution would build character.

Children must understand that many of life's experiences, opportunities, and jobs are only available to individuals who have achieved a high level of expertise. We feel proudest of the achievements for which we have toiled. This is enjoyed in retrospection, for reflecting on past success gives a perpetual sense of satisfaction. New success enhances our self-image and, as excellence begets excellence, new possibilities emerge. Ron Berger said, "Excellence is transformational. Once the child sees what she is capable of, she is never quite the same. There is a new self-image, a new notion of possibility, a new appetite for excellence".[8]

John Hattie is a researcher in education at the University of Melbourne. His "Visible Learning" research is a synthesis of more than 1,200 meta-studies covering more than 80 million students. It represents the largest ever evidence-based research into what works best to improve learning. Considered one of the most influential educators in the world, Hattie argues that teacher expectations of high achievement have the greatest influence on student learning and achievement.[9] The so-called Pygmalion effect was at work in an experiment where teachers were deliberately misinformed that the class they inherited were academically the top-performing, when in fact the sample was purely random. Subsequent tests showed that students in this class achieved significantly higher results than other students pre-tested with the same ability. This is because teachers interact with students differently based on their perception of ability. Teachers who perceive greater potential challenge and encourage those students more, teach them better, have more conversations, and interact on a more mature level. For students, sensing this is powerfully motivating. Hence, teachers and parents must have expectations that all students are capable of progress because, as Hattie says, "having low expectations of a students' success becomes

---
[8] Berger, R. 2003. An Ethic of Excellence. Portsmouth: Heinemann.
[9] Hattie, J. 2009. Visible Learning for Teachers. New York & London: Routledge.

a self-fulfilling prophecy".

Labels are problematic. In fact, not labelling students has a substantial positive influence on learning. Teacher labels include "learning difficulties", the debunked myth of visual, aural or kinaesthetic learners, clumsy, gifted and so on. These all have negative effects. Labels cap potential.

Children can tell when someone doubts their potential. Once this is perceived, they form self-doubt about their ability and capacity for improvement. Children then lose confidence and hope as a learner.

Surprising as this might sound, praise might be the first signal that an adult doubts a child's potential. Being praised for mediocre performance or for simply finishing a task signals low expectations. "The teacher probably praised me for average work because he doesn't think I'm capable of better". The subtleties of teacher-student interactions, whilst unintended by the teacher, are a dead giveaway. But invoking high standards is not enough. Students need to be assured that they can reach those standards, and so they must be taught how to do so. Unsurprisingly, a lack of challenge characterises less effective schools, less effective teachers, and underachievement.

Even though experts attribute their success to the fact that they work and practise much harder than the average person, the public still assumes there is a significant genetic contribution. But the relationship between general intelligence as measured by IQ tests and exceptional performance in any specific domain is weak. Lewis Terman, one of the founders of IQ testing, tracked 1500 child geniuses based on IQ tests. Not one person achieved the expertise or fame he predicted. Geneticist Mae-Wan Ho says "extensive genome-wide scans have failed to find a single gene for intelligence". What does predict lower IQ is social class. Children in low-income families are raised in less stimulating environments. In comparison with children from the top income bracket, Oliver James says, "they have less books, are read to less, taught less math, have much less academic pressure from their parents, and receive five-and-a-half times less encouragement". Where they do spend more time, is in front of a television. Children who choose to limit their television viewing show an improvement in concentration, mood and school behaviour, and become more involved in activities such as music, sports, and reading.[10]

Cross-domain-expertise researchers have come up with a simple yet reliable predictor for expertise: a minimum number of hours required to attain expert status.

---

[10] BBC Newsround. 2007. Kids Live with No TV for 14 days.

3   GOALS

> Genius! For thirty-seven years, I have practised fourteen hours a day, and now they call me a genius.
> (Pablo de Sarasate)

How long does it take to become an expert? Neuroscientist Daniel Levitin says, "The emerging picture is that 10,000 hours of solitary practice is required to achieve the level of mastery associated with being a world-class expert".[11] 10,000 hours of practice amounts to two hours and forty-five minutes of practice per day, every day, for ten years. Daniel Coyle says, "The true expertise of a genius is in their ability to practise obsessively"[12], and Geoffrey Colvin adds: "The conventional wisdom on natural talent is a myth; the real path to great performance is a matter of choice".[13] Listen to experts in our society. They attribute achievement to curiosity, struggle, determination, perseverance, self-discipline, and hard work.

> Thou, O God, who sellest us all good things at the price of labour. (Leonardo da Vinci)

---

[11] Levitin, D. 2006. This Is Your Brain on Music: The Science of a Human Obsession. New York: Penguin.
[12] Coyle, D. 2009. The Talent Code. New York: Bantam Books.
[13] Colvin, G. 2008. Talent is Overrated: What Really Separates World-Class Performers from Everybody Else. London: Nicholas Brealey.

Experts who have invested less than 10,000 hours are rare. For experts in some disciplines, notably virtuosic concert pianists and violinists, the hours required for international expertise are significantly higher. The dexterous physical requirements of these instruments require 20 years or more, accumulating 20-25,000 hours of steady practice to become world class. Inspired by the virtuoso violinist Paganini and determined to develop a technique to match, Franz Liszt practised for up to twelve hours per day, with almost half of this on exercises. Up until his era, there was no record of anyone doing anywhere near this much practice. More recently, a survey at the 2015 Leeds International Piano Competition came up with an average practice quantity among contestants of 25,000 hours.

In *Outliers*, Malcolm Gladwell cites examples of successful people who accumulated 10,000 hours in their formative years. His stories serve to encourage students to appreciate work ethic. Thomas Carlyle (1865) said: "Genius is the infinite capacity to take pains". The pathway to expertise requires too much commitment for most people, so most settle for mediocrity. If it were easy, there would be many more experts.

In 1987, psychologist Anders Ericsson went to Berlin to study expert achievement among graduate violinists. He concluded that the standout reason for the differences in proficiency and achievement was the number of accumulated solitary practice hours. In his famous study, Ericsson listened to and classified these Berlin violinists as world class, very good, competent and amateur, and compared this attainment against the students' quantity of lifetime solitary practice. The correlation was astonishingly predictive. There were no prodigies who reached expertise with less practice. By the age of twenty, the violinists who were classified as world class had practised for at least 10,000 hours, very good 8000 hours, competent not quite 5000 hours, and good amateurs 2000 hours. The connection between expertise and hours practised was established and the "10,000 hours rule" was born.[14]

Ericsson's Study on Berlin Violinists

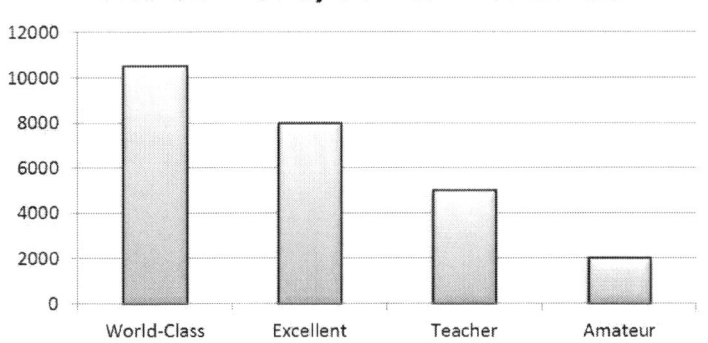

Category	Hours
World-Class	~10500
Excellent	8000
Teacher	5000
Amateur	2000

However, Ericsson clarified the type of practice required to reach this level of excellence. People do not become experts though

---

[14] Ericsson, K. A. Krampe, R. T. and Tesch-Romer, C. 1993. The Role of Deliberate Practice in the Acquisition of Expert Performance. Psychological Review 100: 363–406.

experience alone, nor jamming with others, or going through the motions, but from a system of application he described as "deliberate practice". This is solitary, intense, quality practice, requiring full attention and focus. Like Carlyle's "pain of genius", deliberate practice requires an effort that can be tiring and uncomfortable. Further, to reach expertise, this skill development needs to be achieved in a relatively short, concentrated time frame such as ten years. What people enjoy from this intense work is the progress that leads to excellence. Success flourishes with passion, hard work, support, and opportunity. But it always begins with a goal.

> Most people do not plan to fail, they fail to plan. (John Beckley)

In the 1979 Harvard MBA program, students were asked, "Have you set clear, written goals for your future and made plans to accomplish them?"

84 percent said they had no focussed goals, 13 percent had goals generally in mind, and three percent of graduates had written goals and plans. Ten years later, those students were interviewed again. The 13 percent who had goals generally in mind were earning, on average, twice as much as the 84 percent who had no goals at all. The three percent who had clear, written goals? They were earning, on average, ten times as much as the other 97 percent put together. The

authenticity of this oft-quoted study is dubious; some refer to it as the Yale study, others attribute the year as 1959, and the actual study itself is elusive to find. But the point is - goals are motivational; goals inspire! Setting goals is a great way to fill the mind with positive thoughts. Goals get us off the sofa with the message "back to work!"

There is an old saying: "Life is too short to do what I have to do; it's barely long enough to do what I want to do". We should set genuine, personally significant goals. The goal is personal; an expression of what you genuinely want to achieve. Ask yourself: "Is this something I really want to do? Will I enjoy it, and am I likely to continue to do so in the foreseeable future?" People sometimes choose goals based on what they think they *should* do. Young adults choose goals based upon society's definitions of success and achievement. They succumb to the pressure of what parents, teachers, peers, or significant others think they should do. If goals are not congruent with personal desire, then the pursuit and even the achievement of these goals might lead you further away from what you truly seek. Self-determination requires not only self-perception, but also the ability to resist the social pressures that lead you off course. Parents can help children discover activities they find interesting and enjoyable, and then formulate goals and commit to them.

Many adults encourage students with the goal "just do your best".

But with this remark, the paradox is that students rarely go on to achieve their best. Goal-setting researcher Edwin Locke says "just do your best" goals consistently underperform in comparison to specific and challenging goals. The problem is 1) it is unclear what the target is, 2) any result can fulfil the claim "I did my best" providing a ready excuse and an easy out for lack of accomplishment, and 3) coming from a parent or teacher, it could be perceived as a low expectation. Conversely, John Hattie finds a 250 percent difference in achievement resulting from the most challenging goals to the easiest. Specific, challenging goals, accompanied by the requisite quality and quantity of effort and feedback, leads to greater success.

Lack of proficiency is the primary reason people give up activities, and this can be related to poor goal setting. People sometimes fail to succeed because their goal setting is unrealistic. If we set goals that are much higher than we have previously achieved, we set ourselves up for failure. Conversely, if we keep our sights too low we never will improve substantially enough to enjoy the fruits of increasing complexity. Complex learning requires students to plan, setting short and long-term goals. Long-term goals need to be broken down into mini goals, such as those required when learning a skill.

4   LEARNING SKILLS

One of the frustrations with attempting to learn any new skill is the rate of change of progress. Sometimes the initial period of learning a new skill is quick, and progress is evident. Over time, as progress becomes measured and less clear, children might think they've reached a limit, so they settle for that level, or stop altogether. Plateaus in learning are natural and not indicative of a lack of further potential.

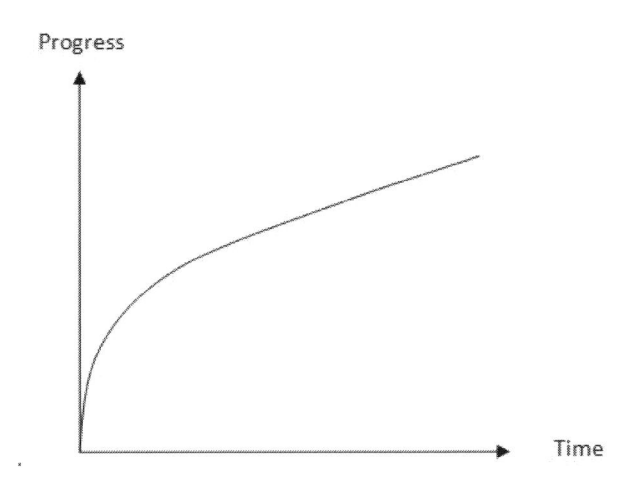

Distributing Practice Over Time

> "Sir, when should I practise?" "Practise only on the days that you eat." (Shin'ichi Suzuki)

Memory is more effective when learning is distributed over a period rather than in one hit. This process of memory consolidation is known as the "spacing effect" and was first recognised more than a century ago. The benefits of the spacing effect apply to so-called "muscle memory" as well as cognitive memory. Hence, skills should be practised regularly for shorter periods (distributed practice) rather than less regularly for longer periods (massed practice). For example, one hour per day for six days a week is more effective than six hours one day per week, and two forty-five-minute sessions per day is more effective than one ninety-minute practice session. The spacing effect aside, effective learning requires 100 percent focus and concentration. Nothing less is acceptable. When this is not being maintained, it's best to stop and regroup. As Ericsson says, "shorter practise sessions with clear goals and 100 percent focus develop skills faster than longer sessions with a 70 percent focus".

Massed practice, like cramming, might be effective for tomorrow's examination or performance, but a considerable memory loss occurs over the days and weeks that follow. Memory formation takes time to make the transition from short-term recall to long-term memory. William James considered cramming a poor way to study and not in accord with how the brain functions:

> Cramming seeks to stamp things in by intense application immediately before the ordeal. But a thing thus learned can form but few associations. On the other hand, the same thing recurring on different days, in different contexts, read, recited on, referred to again and again, related to other things and reviewed, gets well-wrought into the mental structure. This is the reason why you should enforce on your pupils' habits of continuous application. There is no moral turpitude in cramming. It would be the best and the most economical mode of study if it led to the results desired. But it does not.[15]

Distributed practice is more successful for the longer term because between each practice session what has been learned is forgotten at least partially, and must be retrieved. Paradoxically, forgetting is the friend of learning. Forgetting requires relearning, which sets memories more securely. The more times we are required to retrieve or generate answers, the stronger the neural circuitry of the learning becomes. Therefore, rest times between practice sessions are not only important for mental regeneration but also to engage us

---

[15] James, W. 1899. Talks to Teachers on Psychology; and to Students on Some of Life's Ideals. New York: Henry Holt and Company.

in the "forget and retrieve" process. The efficiency of distributed practice means that students should need less total practice time to achieve the same long-term learning results as those yielded by massed practice. Similarly, within a given practice session, skills can be targeted in a blocked or spaced manner.

Blocked and Spaced Repetition Within a Rehearsal

Recently I was watching television when a commercial break interrupted my program. Commercials are annoying at best, but this set of five commercial spots got under my skin. This is because one of the commercials was played three times, not in a row, but with a different commercial in between. Just when I had forgotten it, back it came to haunt me.

A   B   A   C   A

The repeated commercial A was deliberately interspersed with other commercials. The arrangement was cleverly designed to make me forget and retrieve, and I found it difficult to dislodge the commercial from my attention for some time afterward. This marketing technique was so successful, I had learned the commercial. Maybe I can turn this technique to my advantage?

Hermann Ebbinghaus famously revealed the forgetting curve, proposing that students forget 90 percent of what they learn within thirty days. Further to this disheartening finding, the most significant memory loss occurs within the first hour. A memory becomes more robust when the information is repeated in timed intervals. The more repetition cycles, and the more spaces between the repetitions, the more strongly memories are fixed.

Imagine you have thirty minutes available for learning three mini skills. How would you distribute the time? You could work in three blocks consecutively.

Passage A: ten minutes
Passage B: ten minutes
Passage C: ten minutes

Or you could practise in the following manner.

Passage A: four minutes
Passage B: three minutes
Passage A: three minutes
Passage C: four minutes
Passage B: five minutes
Passage A: three minutes
Passage C: six minutes
Passage B: two minutes

The first method is called blocked repetition. The second, like the television commercial example, is known as either spaced repetition, interleaved practice, interspersed practice or a random practice schedule. Blocked repetition refers to sticking to a single practice task until it is effectively learned then progressing to the next learning task. Spaced repetition switches between different tasks during a single practice session. In both methods one encounters the same material for the same amount of overall time but, as with the distributed practice concept, spacing the repetitions exposes one to learning the task repeatedly over a longer time span.

Blocked repetition is a useful technique for creating the neural circuitry for the skill. It is effective for beginners as it allows them to concentrate on a single task. Even for advanced practitioners, very difficult skills require a single focus and attention that might be disrupted if one switches frequently between tasks. Blocked repetition requires the intense engagement of the learner. If concentration wanes, progress can stagnate and possibly decline. It is better to stop and regain focus than to compromise the quality of practice. If the learner has the maturity and patience, spaced repetition is more effective than blocked repetition. As with distributed practice, the benefits of spaced repetition relate to stronger memory formation due to the principle of forgetting and retrieving. Varying practice tasks frequently creates interference, which leads to a degree of forgetting. Returning to the task requires the brain to reconstruct the neuro-physical circuits, leaving a deeper impression on the brain. In practice, though, spaced repetition is difficult, and not recommended for young children. Frequently switching tasks is less intrinsically enjoyable than blocked repetition. It means more frequent failure and more mental effort, which can be frustrating and tiresome. But the reward is that spaced repetition is almost twice as effective as blocked repetition. Marketing teams, professional athletes, ballet dancers and musicians all use spaced repetition to consolidate skills. For example, golfers are required to play shots of varying distances. Whereas blocked repetition drills require a golfer to hit many consecutive balls to one distance marker before aiming at another distance, spaced repetition alternates distance, replicating the real demands of the golf course. I've watched Tiger Woods practise in this manner. In skill-based endeavours, blocked repetition drills can provide a delusion of competence. Most music teachers have heard their students say, "But I could play it yesterday!" The delusion of competence is a reminder that one's own perception of learning can be misleading. As skill-development expert Robert Bjork says, "You look better with the blocked repetition during the training, but you learn better with the spaced repetition".[16]

---

[16] Bjork, R. 2012. The Benefits of Interleaving Practice. Go Cognitive. http://gocognitive.net/interviews/benefits-interleaving-practice

The Learning Power of Repetition

> We are what we repeatedly do; excellence, then, is not an act but a habit. (Aristotle)

Nothing is as important as the quantity and quality of repetition to condition the complex muscle movement required in music and sport. Performing virtuosic music demands some of the most complicated motor patterns imaginable. Anything that occupies working memory reduces the ability to think, so the process of repetition automates these complex motor actions which in turn frees up the brain to concentrate on other considerations such as expression and interpretation. This is essential because at very fast tempos the execution of notes occurs faster than the performer can think about them. Hence, automation enables performance with less conscious effort and greater accuracy. Many activities in daily life are automated through inordinate amounts of repetition. We can all tie shoelaces or do up a neck tie without requiring much concentration. But it takes repeated attempts. To learn a skill, once is never enough.

For a complex skill, it's hard to top the concert pianist. Physiologist Homer Smith cites skilled piano playing as one of the pinnacles of human achievement because of the "demanding muscle coordination of the fingers, which require a precise execution of fast and complex physical movements".[17] Over a lifetime of performance, musicians arguably spend more time in skill acquisition than almost any other group, and thus are studied by neuroscientists for insight into the extraordinary learning capacity of the brain. Consider Frédéric Chopin's popular but challenging *Fantaisie-Impromptu*. This work requires playing approximately 19 notes per second. The performer must learn these notes to such an extent that conscious attention to them is virtually no longer necessary. This is the aim of any playing of music—to render the technical demand to an almost unconscious level. Daniel Levitin says, "Plain old memorization is what musicians do when they learn the muscle movements to play a particular piece". There is nothing necessarily creative about learning the motor mechanics of a phrase; if you repeat an action in a certain manner and for a sustained period of time, the brain will learn, and the muscles obey.

Now the muscle movements have been mastered, the musician can focus to expression. Consideration of tempo, dynamics, tenuto, articulation, and phrasing all combine to transform the notes into music, and the playing becomes less mechanical. A musician who concentrates on mechanics alone cannot be a master.

This is not to underestimate the physical demands of playing 19

---

[17] Smith, H. W. 1961. From Fish to Philosopher. Garden City: Doubleday & Co.

notes per second on the piano. Each finger requires at least two vertical movements as well as lateral ones. Each finger movement involves all three joints, and even motionless fingers are tensed, ready for action. A skilled pianist can perform approximately 380 distinct motor actions per second and still focus on the musicality of the work. This muscle count is calculated before we even get started on other muscular systems in the hands, arms and shoulders. Further, each note must be timed and executed with an individual's interpretative judgment, and when notes are played simultaneously the fingers must differentiate volume levels for acoustic mixing of treble and bass, sometimes accentuating an inner melody. As if this were not enough, the *Fantaisie-Impromptu* requires mastering polyrhythms, meaning two rhythms occurring simultaneously. Almost every bar requires the right hand to play sixteen notes against the left-hand's twelve. This takes some doing. It is a far cry from rubbing your tummy whilst patting your head.

There is no substitute for repetition for developing complex physical skills like playing the piano. The connections between the muscular and neural systems place an extraordinary demand on the hands and fingers. *Fantaisie-Impromptu* is considered difficult but not as fearsome as some works in the literature of piano music. More complicated works have passages that require up to 30 notes per second requiring 600 muscle movements per second, although this does seem to be the upper limit of functional capacity for muscle coordination. The motor cortex is largely dedicated to the small muscles in the fingers, hands, mouth and face. A study of kindergarten children by David Grissmer and colleagues from the University of Virginia concluded that the possession of fine-motor skills which coordinate finger movement with visual perception is one of the strongest predictors of later academic success.[18] The musician is a small muscle super-athlete.

> No other activity we engage in requires the accuracy, speed, timing and smoothness, or coordination of muscular contraction exhibited in finished musical performance. The musician in full flight is an operational miracle. (Frank Wilson)[19]

Achieving a stage of unconscious competence is necessary for complex skills because the storage capacity of the unconscious mind is much greater than that of the conscious mind. Daniel Coyle asserts the unconscious mind can process eleven million pieces of information per second, but the conscious mind is limited to about forty. One achieves unconscious competence in only one way: by

---

[18] Cameron, C. E., Brock, L. L., Murrah, W. M., Bell, L. H., Worzalla, S. L., Grissmer, D. and Morrison, F. J. 2012. Fine Motor Skills and Executive Function Both Contribute to Kindergarten Achievement. Child Development 83(4): 1229–1244.
[19] Wilson, F. R. 1986. Tone Deaf & All Thumbs. Toronto: Viking Books.

repeated practice. The inflexible and automatic knowledge gained through repetition is the foundation of expert performance, but be warned—repeat carefully! The learning brain does not distinguish between good and poor habits but learns whatever we repeat. Repetition creates permanence, and habits are difficult to correct.

Children can struggle with the discipline required for repetition and get lulled into a false sense of mastery when they judge themselves as having mastered a skill reasonably well. Without sufficient repetition, however, the learning will soon unravel.

> If nothing is ever repeated, nothing can ever be known.
> (Heraclitus)

Amateurs stop repeating when they can execute a skill correctly, but it is crucial that they keep repeating after this point. Brain connections represent new learning. Once formed, they strengthen and consolidate with a substance called myelin. Myelin is the white matter of the brain. It insulates the axon sheath of a neuron, increasing the speed and accuracy of data transmission. Myelin transforms performance from clumsy, error-full, slow and difficult, to fluent and effortless. Experts have more myelin build-up on the neural circuits pertinent to their domain than do non-experts. Myelin is a product of activity and is one aspect of brain plasticity, a term that refers to physical changes in the brain. Brain plasticity includes an increase in myelination and an increase in the number of connections between neurons.

> The amateur practises until he gets it right. The professional practises until he cannot get it wrong.
> (Stephen Hillier)

> The amateur stops repeating when he gets it right. The professional repeats well after to consolidate the myelin coating of the axon sheath. (Michael Griffin)

Human nature almost always underestimates how much repetition it takes to master a skill. If a skill thought to be learned yesterday is a muddle today, the student must repeat the repetition process. This can be frustrating, but the process of acquiring skill is not a linear progression. Memories do not just form at the point of learning so it may take several sittings for neural connections to become strong. Some people seem to learn more quickly than others, but learning is not a race, and we are all capable of complex skill development through repetition. Students must learn to be patient and trust in the power of repetition.

> Repetitio est mater studiorum! (Latin proverb: Repetition is the mother of learning!)

Secondly, one must know how to repeat. Our brains crave

newness, so understandably many students find blocked repetition boring and lose focus. Spaced repetition increases the brain's engagement, but repetition also needs variation. Variable repetition maintains the essential nature of the exercise, but it incorporates small changes, for example, shooting for goal from different positions. Novelty enhances memory but requires more conscious engagement on the part of the learner. Repeating material in a variety of ways builds thicker, stronger, and more hardwired connections in the brain. Teachers specialise in designing learning experiences based on variable repetition.

Sleep Learning

> Sleep well, think well. (John Medina)

Sleep expert Dr Matthew Walker has conducted experiments to determine whether humans consolidate learning during sleep. In one study, two groups of subjects practised a typing task using their left hands. The groups practised in the morning and were tested for improvement eight hours later. During the day, one group took a nap of about 75 minutes while the other group stayed awake. For the group that remained awake the test found no significant increase in skill, whereas the group that took a nap recorded a significant increase. NASA also found that having an afternoon nap increased (pilot) performance. Anders Ericsson's study of graduating violinists at the Music Academy of West Berlin found that the highest achievers took more afternoon naps and slept more at night than less accomplished musicians.

Yet another study involved testing pianists to learn a short melody. Subjects in Group A were trained at 10:00 a.m. and tested again at 10:00 p.m. They did not sleep during this time, and no significant improvement in performance was noted. Subjects in Group B were trained at 10:00 p.m. and tested again at 10:00 a.m., following a night of sleep. Performance improved significantly. Many scientific studies reinforce the importance of sleep. One study of 3000 Rhode Island high school students found that students who received A's averaged about fifteen more minutes' sleep than the B students, who in turn averaged fifteen more minutes than the C's. In another study, when players on a Stanford University basketball team increased their sleep time, the team's overall competitive performance improved.

Sleeping does something to improve memory consolidation that being awake does not. Sleep and rest studies confirm that memories do not just form at the point of learning and that the learning brain does not cease activity when practice ends, whether one is asleep or awake. Neural circuitry takes time to form and consolidate, and requires sleep before the full benefit of practice is realised. This knowledge should alleviate some of the frustration students feel when they do not notice immediate improvement after practicing a skill. It also reinforces the importance of getting things right in the first place, prior to rest or sleep. In other words, do not practise mistakes. The deep sleep cycle known as rapid eye movement (REM) seems to be the key for sleep learning to occur. Andrew Bernhard proposes that REM sleep re-energises the brain and replenishes depleted energy reserves in the hippocampus, a major memory storage centre in the brain. Bernhard theorises that REM sleep recharges cerebral glycogen levels, providing critical fuel for the brain. The new reserve of brain energy is stored for use during awake time. This is still just a theory, as scientists do not have a full understanding of the complexities of sleep. However, it seems that during sleep the brain is actively engaged in the repetition and processing of material learned during the day. Conversely, John Medina says the adverse effects of lack of sleep not only thwart memory formation but almost every brain function including attention, logical reasoning, mood, and motor skills.[20]

> We should look at sleep as an active process. Getting enough sleep is a positive thing, which will help you perform in all aspects of life. It may be that extra sleep leads to more effective training routines and helps us

---

[20] Medina, John. 2015. Brain Rules. Seattle: Pear Press.

learn patterns better. (Derk-Jan Dijk, Professor of Sleep and Physiology, University of Surrey)

Chunking

I'll give you ten seconds to memorise and reproduce this list of words: black, flat, criminal, division, table, dog, lawyer, long, little.

How many can you remember?

This is difficult. Why? You might say: "I need more time to engage in repetition to learn this"; or "The words are not connected. They have no meaning"; or "My mind cannot hold this many items on the fly. Now let's rearrange the words.

little black dog   flat table criminal lawyer   long division

Connections between words convert them into phrases, reducing the learning load from nine items to four. Previously the phrase *little black dog* was three separate, unconnected words, but now words relate contextually, becoming one item. This is known as chunking, a mental representation which addresses the limited and fragile nature of short-term memory. By recognising patterns, rules and relationships, we remember more.

Cognitive psychologist George Miller introduced the term

"chunking" in 1956. Miller found that short-term memory could handle only between five and nine discretely different pieces of information at any given moment. For most people this number is closer to six or seven. Chunking increases short-term memory capacity by recoding information. In the exercise above, we connected related words to make short phrases. We chunk when we learn and convey telephone numbers by joining digits together for easier recall. Reading is a form of chunking. Paragraphs, sentences, and punctuation break up information into small units because the reader can only absorb a limited amount of information in a single try. We see words and then sentences rather than individual letters, even if the letters are out of order. "You wulod not blveiee how mcuh my pferaomrcne has iorpmevrd!" Acronyms, abbreviations, and mnemonics are all chunking devices because they make remembering easier by encoding information to assist short-term memory.

Root knowledge is important for chunking. One cannot relate "criminal" and "lawyer" without knowing that a relationship exists between these words. In music theory, being able to find connections and see patterns such as scales and key centres lessens the requirements of memory. Also, the limitation of short-term memory capacity invites us to learn more thoroughly in smaller portions. It also explains the value of making many of our actions, such as basic arithmetic, automatic so we can focus on other things. Successful learners deconstruct key ideas into small bits and practise them repeatedly, and in a variety of ways. Once converted to long-term memory, there seems to be no limit to how much the brain can store, although estimates range anywhere from four terabytes to one million petabytes. Chunking works because so much learning is based on repetition and pattern. That jungle of material looks daunting but, as the chunking process reveals, there is less on the page than meets the eye.

The power of words and concepts helps us to chunk more effectively. Theoretical knowledge in all fields facilitates the identification of patterns providing a detailed frame of reference. The greater the familiarity with patterns, the easier it will be to understand the requirements of the learning.

5 THE TIME THIEF

I did not wish to find when I came to die that I had not lived.

(Henry David Thoreau)

Studies of elderly persons find that many regret not having engaged in more active recreation. Learning a musical instrument, a sport such as scuba diving or golf, establishing better relationships and participating in art, drama, or writing are some of the most cited activities people would like to have pursued. The least common responses include spending more hours at the office, reading more gossip magazines, and watching more television. Television, however, still gets the lion's share of children's leisure time.

Generations of adults spend years participating in inactive leisure pursuits that dull the senses, when they could be learning and applying skills. Ken Robinson's distinction between leisure and true recreation compares the "effortless and passive nature of leisure with the re-creating action of recreation".[21] Just as physical and mental effort energises recreation, too much passive leisure can be draining. Our consumerist and commercial media lobby on behalf of Passive Entertainment, Incorporated. They beguile us to seek happiness through external means, usually requiring us to part with our cash, in

---

[21] Robinson, K. 2009. The Element. New York: Viking.

lieu of personal effort. To counterbalance this, parents and teachers must educate children in the benefits of activity and involvement. Kahlil Gibran wrote in his 1923 philosophical classic The Prophet:

> Or have you only comfort, and the lust for comfort, that stealthy thing that enters the house a guest, and becomes a host, and then a master?
> Ay, and it becomes a tamer, and with hook and scourge makes puppets of your larger desires.
> Though its hands are silken, its heart is of iron.
> It lulls you to sleep only to stand by your bed and jeer at the dignity of the flesh.
> Verily the lust for comfort murders the passion of the soul, and then walks grinning in the funeral.

The systematic time investment required for learning can be stolen by time thieves, and television is one of the greatest offenders. After work and sleep, television consumes the most time and attention. On average, people watch three hours per day. For many, this is half of their available leisure time and accumulates to ten years spent in front of the television in an 80-year lifespan. Watching television can help one feel relaxed and passive. Turn off the television, though, and the sense of relaxation ends, but feelings of sluggishness continue. "The television has absorbed viewers' energy," says Mihaly

Csikszentmihalyi, "leaving them fatigued, disheartened, and after large quantities of viewing, slightly depressed".[22] People also report more difficulty concentrating after watching television. It's not just watching television that's at issue. One American study found that children are exposed to on average almost four hours of background television each day, and the youngest – under the age of two – five-and-a-half hours per day. The impact from this includes a growing tendency to become bored easily, and an inability to pay attention. If you are not watching the television, turn it off! Australian health regulations recommend no television for infants under the age of two, less than one hour per day for older children, and two hours for adults.

> I find television very educational. Every time someone switches it on, I go into another room and read a good book. (Groucho Marx)

Television is a wonderful multimedia art form capable of educating and amusing us. The problem lies in the vast number of hours people spend watching it. Television viewing can turn into an addiction. When television interferes with the ability and desire to learn new things, to participate in active life, and to commit to music

---

[22] Csikszentmihalyi, M. 1990. Flow: The Psychology of Optimal Experience. New York: Harper Perennial.

practice, there is clearly a problem. Excess television viewing dehumanises; it acts as a parasite of the mind. Not only does it dull the mind, but it also steals time from our lives.

> It is in the improvident use of leisure that the greatest wastes of life occur. (Robert Park)

Television is not the only time thief. In one Australian study, 80 percent of school students reported distraction and procrastination due to the time they spend on Facebook. A Stanford University study found that multi-taskers are distracted more easily, have poorer concentration, work less efficiently, and do not write as well. We can't parallel process, we can only think about one thing at a time. When people think they are multi-tasking, they are in fact switching between thoughts very quickly, causing a divide in attention. However, students who uni-task, that is, immerse themselves in one thing at a time, remember their work better, get more done, and their work is usually more creative and of higher quality. Put aside distractions and focus on one task at a time. Attending to e-mail, inseparable in many people's business and social organisations, is another time thief. An Australian investigation found that "Workers spend on average 14.5 hours per week checking, reading, deleting, arranging, and responding to e-mail".[23]

> The future will belong not only to the educated, but to those educated to use leisure wisely. (Charles K. Brightbill)

Computer games are more interactive than watching television, but the creative aspect is mostly reactive and responsive rather than self-initiated, because most computer games generate play content that must be followed. A Carnegie-Mellon study found that by the time a boy turns twenty-one he is likely to have spent about 10,000 hours playing computer games. This is the same amount of time the average student spends in school from the fifth grade to twelfth grade. It is also the same amount of time required to develop an expertise. A Ministry of Japan study found an 18 percent differential in math results comparing students who played computer games for four hours with those who played for one hour. The Japanese government now recommends no-computer-games days for students. Similarly, a Cambridge University study linked more screen time with lower school grades. Most people underestimate their phone touching. The average person touches and swipes 2617 times per day, equating to 145 minutes in 76 separate sessions a day, and the top 10 per cent do 5427 touches per day. 80 percent of phone interaction is with games. Including television, computer games, and social

---

[23] Australian Daily Telegraph, 2008

networking sites, children aged eight to eighteen spend approximately 6.75 hours per day in front of a screen. What is the return on this time investment? The use of leisure time can be a matter of balance. We all need to wind down. To relax and just be is important. We are human beings, not human doings, but if passive leisure is the single object of recreation, its pursuit can become meaningless. The effects of passive leisure are ephemeral, but recreation has meaning for the long-term. It is surprising that, with so many opportunities for recreation and leisure, enjoyment can be elusive. For a world obsessed with work, leisure is a serious matter, and learning how to use leisure time has become a significant challenge. To enjoy leisure, a degree of effort and challenge is necessary.

The movie Dead Poets Society, with its life-force motto Carpe diem, offers a powerful message for teenagers. Robin Williams's character, Mr Keating, emboldens his students to think independently, to be wary of conformist pressure, and to use their precious leisure time to "suck the marrow out of life". Robert Herrick's poem "To the Virgins, to Make Much of Time" appears in the film and underscores its message of the importance of seizing the day.

> GATHER ye rosebuds while ye may,
> Old time is still a-flying:
> And this same flower that smiles to-day

To-morrow will be dying.
The glorious lamp of heaven, the sun,
The higher he's a-getting,
The sooner will his race be run,
And nearer he's to setting.
That age is best which is the first,
When youth and blood are warmer;
But being spent, the worse and worst
Times still succeed the former.
Then be not coy, but use your time,
And while ye may go marry:
For having lost but once your prime
You may forever tarry.

6 THE METASKILLS OF ACHIEVEMENT

Skill development increases in accordance with the quantity and quality of practice time. Achievement in any domain, however, is underpinned by another set of core skills. Why is it that some people are motivated to work harder and longer? How do they ignore distractions? How can teachers and parents instill a mindset of determination, perseverance, and self-discipline in their children? First and foremost is motivation.

Motivation

> Nothing great was ever achieved without enthusiasm.
> (Ralph Waldo Emerson)

Motivation, from the Latin movere meaning to move, is the fuel that starts, stops, directs and sustains human behaviour. It creates a desire to persist beyond the boundaries of comfort, to overcome obstacles, and to achieve beyond our own, and others', highest expectations. Motivation gets results. It is an overarching concern for parents.

In general terms, motivation is categorised as either intrinsic or extrinsic. When we enjoy an activity for what it is and for the pleasure it brings, we are self-motivated, or intrinsically motivated. The reward for doing the activity comes from the activity itself. With extrinsic motivation, the reward is an external benefit from doing the activity. We observe intrinsic motivation when children engage in activities alone, when they choose to participate in activities without external pressure, and when they engage in activities in the absence of the promise of or opportunity for external reward. It is not only the choice to engage in activity that defines intrinsic motivation, but also the quality of that involvement. Trying hard and spending extra time on a task are examples of intensity and persistence. These are hallmarks of an intrinsically motivated student.

Extrinsic motivation is entrenched in systems of education. External rewards—including gold stars, stickers, and grades—are both material and verbal and presented with the hope that students will be encouraged to learn. In his massive body of research, John Hattie found "praise, punishment and extrinsic rewards are the most ineffective forms of feedback for enhancing achievement". External motivation tends to be transient in that students are likely to lose their motivation when the prospect of an external reward disappears. Extrinsic performance goals and intrinsic learning goals are different. Getting an A in math class is an extrinsically motivated performance goal, whereas becoming a better mathematician is a learning goal. This is one of the drawbacks of grading systems. Students are interested in achieving good grades but become less interested in learning because of being graded. When students focus on grades they do the work that is necessary to get that grade, but rarely more. When told that work will be graded, students are less likely to enjoy the task and less likely to return to that material after the test. In comparison to learning goals, outcomes from performance goals are shallow and limited. Also, striving for good grades can lead to overly conformist behaviour as students try to please the teachers who are grading them. Grades that separate attainment and effort are also problematic. If incongruent, they can signal a fixed genetic disposition. High grade low effort indicates you are a natural, you don't have to try hard and can still achieve good grades. Low grade high effort suggests you have no real ability. Effort is hopeless. If effort does not correlate with improvement, then the quality of effort must be examined.

Another problem with grading is the subjective nature of the assessor. Especially with divergent, expressive and creative tasks, teachers differ widely in evaluation. Compounding this problem is the so-called halo effect. Unconscious teacher bias favours attractive students, and those labelled as gifted. Attractive students are perceived as smarter than their less attractive peers. One study found that on a scale of one to five, with five being most attractive, students ranked a four were being graded 36 percent higher in tests than students with an attractiveness score of two. Students perceived as attractive receive more opportunities, more attention, and more positive encouragement from teachers, as do students labelled as gifted. Studies confirm that parents also show bias and, whether they acknowledge it or not, children perceive the bias.

Intrinsic interest sustains motivation. We are born curious, with a natural desire to seek out novelty and challenge, to exercise our abilities, and to explore. Have you ever seen an infant who was not curious and self-directed? Extrinsic rewards can deliver short-term boosts. They can serve as a last resort to kindle a desired behaviour, or as a symbol of competence and belonging, but the effect wears off and can reduce longer-term motivation. Parents should use rewards cautiously. Rewards are often used to persuade people to do things they otherwise would not do. Unless perceived by the recipient as a source of information regarding competence, offering a reward conveys a message that the task is not inherently enjoyable. Daniel Pink says, "Pay your son to take out the trash and you've pretty much guaranteed he will never do it again for free".[24] Once you offer a reward for undertaking an activity there is no going back. I suspect my parents grasped this when they raised us children. My siblings and I received a little pocket money, but this was not connected to the expectation that we help with household chores. As Confucius taught, neither punishments nor rewards teach people virtue.

In Punished by Rewards, Alfie Kohn says that children who are driven by extrinsic motivators never develop the natural curiosity and desire for self-fulfillment required to engage in deep learning. Kohn argues that, aside from failing to motivate, contingent rewards "kill creativity, undermine interest, fail to alter the attitudes behind learning behavior, and rupture relationships". Contingent rewards are based on performance outcomes, namely, *if you do this, I will give you that*. Harvard Business School's Teresa Amabile declares that rewards are particularly detrimental for creative tasks:

> Managers in successful, creative organizations rarely offer specific extrinsic rewards for outcomes. However, they freely

---

[24] Pink, D. 2009. Drive: The Surprising Truth About What Motivates Us. New York: Riverhead Books.

and generously recognise creative work by individuals and teams—often before the ultimate commercial impact of those efforts is known.

However, rewards are effective when offered unexpectedly after completion of a task. Celebrating after the outcome does not undermine learning because it recognises and feeds back competence. This eliminates the if…then… condition to act. There are other exceptions where contingent rewards might be appropriate. Some enjoyable activities require an initial effort that may not be naturally enjoyable and therefore might benefit from incentives to initiate the first stage of learning. This is sometimes the case when very young children are coming to terms with the peculiar technical demands of an instrument such as the violin.

Intrinsic motivation is strongly linked with higher quality learning. Therefore, a central mission for parents is to influence how children motivate themselves. Only then will children freely apply the effort required to reach greater heights. A model of intrinsic motivation that has influenced more research than any other comes from the University of Rochester. Since the early 1970s, Edward Deci and Richard Ryan have tested and refined ideas about motivation, resulting in a concise tripartite model of intrinsic motivation.

Their theory is based on three innate human needs: the need to belong, the need to feel competent, and the need to direct one's own actions.

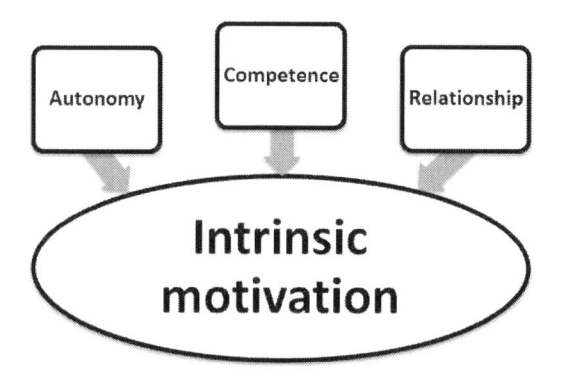

[Diagram: Autonomy, Competence, Relationship → Intrinsic motivation]

Autonomy

> We are most engaged and do our best work when we act according to our own will. (Richard Ryan)

Autonomy refers to actions chosen and endorsed by self. The key here is *choice*. Increasing a child's options and choices is more likely to foster intrinsic motivation and subsequent effort. As early and as often as possible, parents should give children some control of their actions. More generally, children have too little choice regarding what they learn. In his book *Overschooled but Undereducated: How the crisis in education is jeopardizing our adolescents,* UK educator John Abbott says that children have no choice in approximately 75 percent of primary school learning activities. Children are always requesting to do things their own way, and they do not like being forced to conform any more than adults do.

Autonomy refers to an internal sense of control. That is, how do my actions and my effort determine outcomes? The alternative to this is external control. One strand of thinking about autonomy is attribution theory. Attribution justifies an outcome. For example, a student response for failing an exam might be:

- I'm just not good at this subject (lack of ability).
- I failed because I'm dumb (lack of ability).
- I didn't study very much (lack of effort).
- I didn't study properly (lack of strategy).
- It was too hard (task difficulty).
- I was unlucky (lack of good fortune).
- I just had an off day (lack of good fortune).
- People were noisy (the fault of others).
- I wasn't taught this (the fault of others).

Attribution can explain why some students quit whereas others work harder on a task. Students who attribute success and failure to effort and strategy are more persistent than students who attribute success and failure to external factors, such as talent.

Attribution theory asks the question "why am I good at what I do?" For example, the question might be "why am I good at music?" Consider three responses:

1. I was born this way. I got lucky in the genetic lottery and have a special innate musical gift.
2. I have a good teacher. My teacher tells me "I will make you a fine musician".
3. I work at it. I practise hard, I seek advice, and I learn from my mistakes. My effort is the primary reason for my progress.

The first two responses attribute competency to factors outside of one's control. This undermines autonomy, which in turn lowers intrinsic motivation. The third response supports autonomy. Students with this type of attribution ultimately learn better.

Praise

In the main, it is the subtleties of praise that develop a fixed mindset. Motivational interventions that control or coerce behaviour include contingent rewards and the "praise" type of verbal feedback. The functional significance of feedback is dependent upon the perception of the child. Feedback that is informational and related to competence is incredibly important and highly motivational. For example, "your right foot is in the correct position for the backhand" refers to an important attribute of the tennis stroke. Whereas "I really like it when you sit quietly and don't talk" will be perceived as an attempt to control behaviour.

To reach goals, quality feedback is paramount. But preceding adult feedback, children need an opportunity to self-evaluate. "What do you think?" Feedback is most effective when consistent and accurate, quick and frequent. It needs to be specific. Giving positive feedback does not necessarily mean praising. Nor do students need praise to develop a healthy self-view. Tim Gallwey says, "Compliments are criticisms in disguise because both are used to manipulate behaviour".[25] This reasoning implies, "if he likes me for doing well, he might dislike me for not doing well". Praise and criticism are part

---

[25] Gallwey, T. W. 1974. The Inner Game of Tennis. New York: Random House.

of the same continuum of judgement.

It is important to identify what is being praised and why it is being praised. If an activity makes children happy they do not need adults to intervene. As with tangible rewards, there is a danger that children will shift the intention of their actions off the activity and towards the praise. Children respond to adult praise because they are hungry for approval, but praise can lead to a dependency on the approval of others, and can ultimately result in insecurity. Commenting on the process or the result rather than the person avoids the problem of the personal judgement inherent in most praise. "That's a beautiful song" is preferable to "You're such a good songwriter". The latter draws attention to the self and contains no useful information for improving or confirming the process and skill within the task. A comment like "your hard work and attention to details has significantly improved your performance" refers to effort and process. Emphasising achievement through effort fosters a growth intelligence mindset, but "you're so talented, you always learn quickly" might lead a child to think that not learning quickly is a sign of lack of talent.

A useful indirect approach in giving positive feedback is to frame it within a question. "How did you manage to play the music so fluently?" To encourage, praise is unnecessary. Taking interest, smiling, expressing enthusiasm, asking questions and providing positive feedback are the best forms of encouragement. Praise is a lazy utterance in comparison with the thought and consideration required to encourage. Adults must think through their motives in saying what they say and then consider how to phrase their words so children do not interpret it as an evaluation. "Sticks and stones may break my bones but words can cause irreparable damage".

Children can be quick to apply the language of absolutes, suffocating learning potential. Words like "never" and "always" pose a problem. Whether it's "I've never been any good at mathematics", or "I always play badly in public", parents should re-phrase this language of limitation as quickly as possible. Enter the most powerful word in the growth mindset vocabulary: "yet". Rather than accept utterances of permanent incapacity and failure, re-phrase the self-evaluation with the word yet attached. When a student said to me "I'm just no good at reading", I replied "Not true, Simon. We can all improve if we know how, and I'm going to give you strategies to improve. Now repeat after me: I'm not good at reading – yet". This conveys to children that we believe they can make progress with practice and effort. Failure is rarely caused by lack of aptitude. But it is confirmed when people quit.

Feedback is more effective when correct processes are positively reinforced prior to incorrect processes. For example, rather than "no, that's not right" affirm the parts of the process that are being attended to well, and then refer to the areas that require more work. In doing so, be careful with conjunctions "but" and "however" as these can undermine the positive message. Feedback needs to entice children to work in a new way. When offering critical suggestions, preface remarks with "I wouldn't be giving you this feedback if I didn't think you were capable of using it to improve". Also, "you might" promotes more autonomy than "you should".

Boys' education expert Ian Lillicoe recommends praising a boy through touch, such as giving him a pat on the back. In some societies, a sense of touch has been lost, as society has become paranoid about it. But boys connect with one another in a very physical way.

Albert Einstein was skeptical about the merits of praise, saying "The only way to escape the personal corruption of praise is to go on working". Many people are uncomfortable with the evaluative and judgmental aspects of praise. Some find it condescending. Jimi Hendrix said "I don't consider myself to be the best, and compliments distract me". Perhaps these men, despite being at the top in their respective fields, observed an erosion of work ethic attributable to the praise from others. Extrinsic motivators can destroy intrinsic motivation; the two coexist uncomfortably.

> Two kinds of motivation are not better than one.
> Extrinsic will always erode intrinsic. (Alfie Kohn)[26]

Why do we hang on to ideas even though they don't work or at best are ineffective? Many adults intuitively believe that praise leads to high self-esteem and a feeling of specialness, which in turn results in greater prospects for success and happiness. But the evidence does not support this. Links between high self-esteem and academic performance are questionable at best and contribute to lower academic achievement at worst. High self-esteem does not reduce

---

[26] Kohn, A. 1993. Punished by Rewards. Boston: Houghton Mifflin.

anxiety. In *Self-Compassion*, Kristin Neff says that "self-esteem is a side-effect of success, the consequence of healthy behaviour rather than the cause. Success leads to self-esteem, not the other way around, and artificially boosting it doesn't work". This has support from Carol Dweck: "It's a mistake to believe that you can simply hand children self-esteem by telling them how smart and talented they are. We cannot boost children's self-esteem by protecting them from failure".

Artificial attempts to boost self-esteem can result in self-absorption, an overreliance on praise and reward, grade inflation, and a need to see ourselves as better than others. Seeking high self-esteem leads to comparison, excluding 50 percent of people from being above average. Most parents like to think of their children as being special, and tell them so regularly. Unique is one thing, but children interpret *special* as being better than others, and this can cause narcissism.

Regrettably, most schools and teachers are not familiar with the research on praise and self-esteem. They assume that using praise to lift self-esteem can only be a good thing. Dweck refers to one study where the students doing the least amount of homework and receiving the lowest grades were receiving by far the most praise. This might convey to the student "you're probably not very smart so congratulations on reaching this mediocre level". Excess praise can cause low achievers who exert little effort to believe that they are as competent as the higher achievers, resulting in an impression that they have little need to improve their performance. Praising students regardless of their performance encourages a belief that effort doesn't matter.

It is likely that this view of the impact of praise is new to the reader, and I understand it might be difficult to digest. Sit with it a while. It takes courage to consider new ideas and to reconsider assumptions. Well-intentioned though it might be, unearned praise and over-praise from adults does not produce the desired long-term outcomes.

> The problem with some school-based methods to boost self-esteem is they don't distinguish between healthy and unhealthy self-esteem. Teachers use indiscriminate praise, focussing on the child's level of self-esteem, not on why or how it gets there. Thus, many children come to believe they deserve compliments no matter what they do. - Kirstin Neff[27]

Furthermore, in a *Wall Street Journal* article Kay Hymowitz writes:

> And what do 15,000 studies show? High self-esteem doesn't improve grades, reduce anti-social behaviour, deter alcohol drinking or do much of anything good for kids. In fact, telling kids how smart they are can be counterproductive. Many children who are convinced that they are little geniuses tend not to put much effort into their work. Others are troubled by the anxiety of adults who feel it necessary to praise them

---

[27] Neff, Kristin. 2011. Self-Compassion. London: Hodder & Stoughton.

constantly.[28]

Iain McGilchrist supports this view: "high self-esteem is positively correlated with a tendency to be unrealistic, to take offence too easily, and to become violent and demanding if one's needs are not met".[29]

High self-esteem and healthy self-esteem are not the same thing. One study found that school athletes who received the most praise from their coaches in time became least confident in their athletic skills. This may seem counter-intuitive, but the reasons explaining it are logical. Superfluous praise can be interpreted by a student as indicative of low expectation; that little more improvement is expected of them. Similarly, students interpret teacher sympathy or pity in response to failure as indicative of lack of ability.

The alternative is to encourage persistence and examination of learning strategies: "How did you prepare for this? What could you do differently next time? Let's learn from this so we can improve". Praise can lull children into accepting lower standards, and mislead them into thinking they are doing better than they are. Over-the-top compliments can be received as patronising and an insult to one's capability. Critical feedback, though, sends the message that one is capable of better performance. Whilst the link between self-esteem and achievement is weak, the link between autonomous competence,

---

[28] Hymowitz, K. 2009 What the Experts Are Saying Now. Wall Street Journal. August 25.
[29] McGilchrist, I. 2009. The Master and his Emissary: The Divided Brain and the Making of the Western World. New Haven, CT: Yale University Press.

or self-efficacy, and achievement is the most powerful.

Relationships

Positive relationships profoundly influence student motivation and learning. School attendance, attitude, emotional engagement and general academic achievement all improve when students perceive acceptance, support, and encouragement from parents and teachers.

> They don't care how much you know until they know how much you care. (Theodore Roosevelt)

When students connect with and respect their teacher, they are more likely to subscribe to the values and practices of that teacher. If the student does not like the teacher, very often they will not do well in that subject. Some evidence suggests this is particularly so for boys. If girls like a subject, even if not the teacher, they are more likely to prevail.

> Boys learn teachers. Boys will work hard for a teacher they like. (Steve Biddulph)

Teresa Amabile was researching motivation among senior business executives. She expected recognition to be the number one motivational force. No doubt, recognition is one of the strongest motivational forces for children. However, Amabile found an even stronger motivator: making progress.[30] People love to get better at

---

[30] Amabile, T. and Kramer, S. J. 2011. The Power of Small Wins. Harvard Business Review 89(5): 70–80. https://hbr.org/2011/05/the-power-of-small-wins

what they do.

Competence

Progress is the great motivator. It is central to intrinsically driven learning. Even if children have healthy self-esteem, are interested in the learning content, and believe it to be important, they will not fully engage if they believe the task beyond them. Hence the number one reason people quit learning? Lack of progress resulting in fragile competence beliefs.

> "I'm not getting any better."
> "I'm no good at this."
> "I just can't do it."

Progress cultivates pride, enthusiasm and perseverance. Children need the tools for making progress. A practice system that incorporates repetition, chunking and slow physical movement, when done on a regular basis over time, will deliver progress. When students quit learning, they give reasons like "(the activity) was boring, I can't be bothered", or "it's stupid". Children use words like boring to protect self-image, ego, and lack of effort. Devaluing an activity allows one to quit without the embarrassment of failing. Kristin Neff puts it well:

> One way to increase self-esteem is to value the things we are good at and devalue the things we are bad at. The problem here is that we may undercut the importance of learning valuable skills just because it makes us feel better about

ourselves. In other words, our desire to achieve high self-esteem in the short term may harm our development in the long run.

The real reason for quitting is fragile competence beliefs. And this almost always points to a lack of practice time with the skill, poor goal setting, or poor practice methods.

Optimal Challenge and Flow

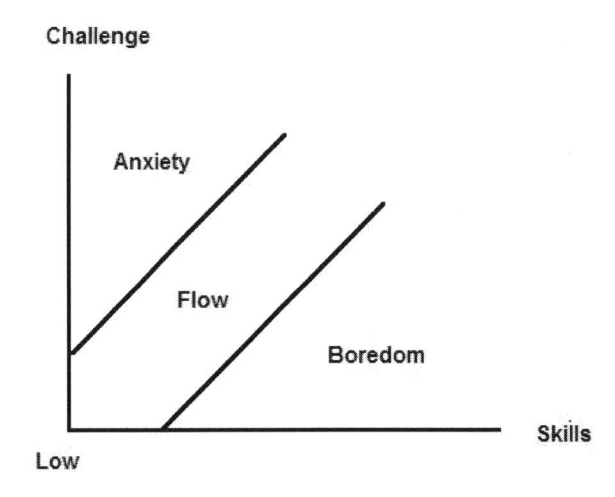

```
Challenge
   |
   |        Anxiety
   |             /   /
   |            /   /
   |           /   /
   |          / Flow /
   |         /   /
   |        /   /   Boredom
   |       /   /
   |_____/___/_____ Skills
Low
```

Like with goal setting, the best challenges are positioned at the edge of, or just beyond, our present skill level. Requiring intense focus and concentration, our ability is stretched and we emerge from the challenge with greater skill and a deep sense of accomplishment. This describes flow. Competitive situations are a great way to achieve flow. Take, for instance, a tennis match between closely matched opponents. Both players find flow because the contest has the right amount of tension between challenge and skill, requiring total immersion in the activity.

To achieve the flow state, the challenge must be significant enough to increase skills, but still be in reach of present ability. We grow little from goals set too low, or too high. Being just out of our present grasp, this optimum improvement zone requires effort and struggle. You do not get fit without some discomfort. The young boy who catches a ball at six feet will seek to increase the distance to eight feet. He deliberately places himself back into a position of incompetence to manufacture a greater challenge to overcome.

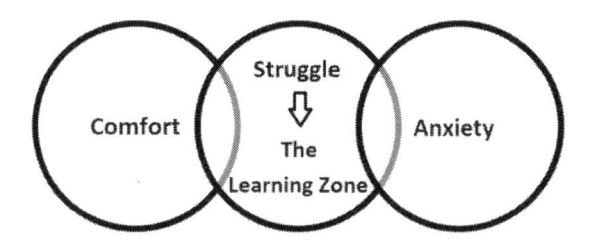

The Learning Zone

> It is doubtful whether any heavier curse could be
> imposed on man than the complete gratification of all
> his wishes without effort on his part, leaving nothing for
> his hopes, desires, or struggles. (Samuel Smiles)

When I was a boy I enjoyed playing table tennis with my father. Even though he was better than me, the competition was good for both of us. How so? Perhaps my father went easy, allowing me to win some points? No, even young children have pride, and I would not accept having my father throw a game. He in fact used his weaker hand to deliberately reduce his skill level, enabling a more even contest for both of us. Flow experiences are created by manipulating the challenge and skills axes, per the graph above.

> Our antagonist strengthens our nerves and sharpens our skills. (Edmund Burke)

Flow offers some of life's peak experiences because they involve personal growth and self-awareness. Flow represents a style of learning that deliberately regulates, and reflects on challenges resulting in increased ability.

The best sporting contests are close games, providing optimal challenge. The problem with competition is when it directs energy from the process to the prize. Genuine joy in competition comes from the knowledge that we are getting better. The Latin phrase *con petire* (to seek together) sums this up well; we seek to actualise one another's potential. As well as competing with others, competition includes competing against a personal best, or external benchmark such as passing an exam.

The primary appeal of computer games is that they generate flow. Computer games quickly determine a player's ideal level of challenge, and once this level is mastered the game increases the challenge in small increments. As the difficulty increases, so does the skill of the player. In the flow mindset, if you are the smartest person in the room, then you are in the wrong room. Like the child who increases his ball-catching distance, experts deliberately increase the difficulty of a challenge. Professional golfers practise the hardest shots, and footballers try to kick goals from impossible angles. No matter what the activity, we can contrive the challenge to create flow.

There are other ways to contrive difficulty. When I was a teenager, my mother set up a meeting with Adelaide musician Bruce Raymond because she was worried I was losing interest in playing the piano. Bruce told me he practised the trumpet at 5:00 a.m. He believed that if he could master his trumpet on chilly Adelaide winter mornings, he would have the confidence to play at any time of day. He deliberately chose difficult practice conditions. This inspired me. I learned to welcome the piano with stiff keys and morning-cold fingers, knowing these conditions could only make me stronger if I approached difficulty with the same attitude as Bruce.

> Enjoyment does not depend on what you do but how you do it. (Mihaly Csikszentmihalyi)

Education gives us freedom of the mind. A goal of education is to inculcate an autotelic and learning-for-life mindset. A survey of 55,000 students at tertiary institutions in Australia and New Zealand conducted by the Australian Council for Educational Research showed that roughly 33 percent of students intended to drop out of their degree program after the first year. The number one reason stated was boredom. Given that resources for self-learning have never been greater, this reflects poorly on our education system.

Boredom leads to sensationalism. The newness of things loses its sheen very quickly, providing conditions ripe for exploitation by the consumer marketing industry. Iain McGilchrist explains:

> Pop-culture is full of vibrancy and vitality, but its condition is one of boredom. Boredom is accompanied by an appetite for the new and the different, and novel excitement. This condition signifies a lack of imagination and without imagination, crude sensationalism is all that remains. There is a vicious cycle between feelings of boredom, emptiness and restlessness, on the one hand, and gross stimulation and sensationalism on the other. Whenever boredom reigns, speech becomes gross and hyperbolic, music loud and nervous, and actions bizarre and foolish. Advertising is connected to this. It has much to answer for shaping this mass-market culture.

Enjoyment

> Human beings seek self-esteem and happiness more than anything else. (Aristotle)

Motivated learners are curious. They keep exploring and ask a lot of questions. They are born eager to gain new knowledge of the world, and of their self. We observe this eagerness by catching a glimpse of children who are visibly delighted by learning something new. One of the clearest indicators of a motivated student is whether they enjoy the activity. Enjoyment is more than an ephemeral feeling. It nourishes brains and bodies and fosters better interpersonal relationships. Happy people are more helpful and cooperative. Happy children pay more attention in the classroom, learn better, and think more creatively. Dale Carnegie said, "People rarely succeed unless they enjoy what they are doing".

> Whilst happiness is sought for its own sake, every other goal—health, beauty, money, or power—is valued only because we expect it will make us happy. Enjoyment is characterised by a sense of accomplishment. A person can feel pleasure without any effort, but it is impossible to enjoy an activity unless attention is fully concentrated on that activity. The self does not grow as a consequence of pleasurable experiences. (Mihaly Csikszentmihalyi)

Self-Discipline

> If IQ was the biggest social construct of the twentieth century, then self-discipline is the biggest construct of the twenty-first century. (Stuart Shanker)

In 1972 Walter Mischel and colleagues performed an experiment on the self-regulation capability of four-year-old children. Each child was given a marshmallow and told that if they could refrain from eating it for fifteen minutes, they would get an additional marshmallow. Not willing to wait, two out of three children gobbled their marshmallow. Fifteen years later the children were re-examined. The children who, when aged four, could refrain from eating the marshmallow for the future benefit of a second were more successful on a number of measures than those who had succumbed to temptation.

Children able to delay gratification are more popular, earn better grades, and had an average of 210 more points on their SAT tests.

Another study, this time by Angela Duckworth and Martin Seligman with eighth grade students, compared the roles of IQ and self-discipline in predicting academic achievement. Self-discipline was the clear winner.[31] Further, Martin Westwell said "the ability to resist impulse at age 10 is a better predictor of earning power at age 30, than numeracy skills age 10". It is self-control rather than IQ that predicts fewer absences from school, more time spent studying, and less time watching television. In an age in which children encounter endless social media distraction, the ability to focus on a difficult task becomes increasingly important for success.

The ability to resist impulse is an executive function, and is critical for life success. Human weakness creates a continuous struggle for control of our desires. We make annual resolutions to be more financially responsible, to live more healthily, and to be more productive. Our craving for immediate pleasures is evident in the credit card industry. Lack of personal control is the source of debt, obesity and general misery. Self-control is essential for high achievement, but it requires effort and sacrifice. For those with the will, the ability to resist impulse for immediate gratification pays a handsome dividend.

---

[31] Duckworth, A. L. and Seligman, M. E. 2005. Self-Discipline Outdoes IQ in Predicting Academic Performance of Adolescents. Psychological Science 16: 939–944.

> You should never give up what you want most, for what you want in the moment. (Gloria Perkins to her son, Olympic champion Kieran Perkins)

With so many diversions competing for attention, children must develop a capacity for singular focus. For success, resisting impulse is essential. In Emotional Intelligence, Daniel Goleman says "there is perhaps no psychological skill more important than resisting impulse".

Attitude and Perseverance

> The greatest discovery of my generation is that humans can alter their lives by altering their attitude of mind. If you change your mind, you can change your life. (William James)

Attitude can determine the consequences of a predicament and can even transform what seems to be a crisis into an opportunity. Indeed, the Chinese character for crisis includes both danger and opportunity. Parents can help children find this inner resolve for those times when work becomes difficult. They should find examples that students can relate to, including:

- personal and peer examples.
- parent/significant adult examples.
- historical-figure examples.

Have students reflect on past experiences when they have

persevered to overcome difficulties. Ask them to consider how they felt. What was the outcome? Was it worth it? Personal experience is a great educator. Putting children in touch with their resolve empowers them to overcome trying times in the future. Second to personal experience, the examples of peers of a similar age are highly influential. children often think, if she can do this, then maybe I can. Thirdly, the personal examples of significant adults, such as teachers and parents, guide and inspire children. Infused in the power of a story, anecdotes of adults' trials and tribulations and how they overcame them can captivate children. Finally, historical examples of courage and determination abound to inspire us all.

Ludwig van Beethoven provides one of the most stirring examples of courage and fortitude in the face of personal disaster. The most renowned composer of his day—and perhaps of all time—Beethoven, in his mid-twenties, became aware of problems with his hearing. Over the next few years, and after many consultations with his doctors, it became clear that he was headed for a life without sound. Feeling hopeless, he even considered suicide. But, reaching deep into his spirit, Beethoven resolved to continue living for his art. He changed his attitude and hence his life. "I will not endure this! I will seize fate by the throat," he proclaimed. "Most assuredly it shall not get me wholly down. I will struggle with this fate; it shall never drag me down".[32] Beethoven continued to compose, and his output during this difficult period includes some of the greatest music ever written.

---

[32] Beethoven wrote "The Heiligenstadt Testament" in October 1802.

Winston Churchill was another who formed the ability to prosper in difficult situations. "When things are going well he is good, but when things are going badly he is superb!" said General Hastings Ismay, Churchill's chief military assistant. Successful people don't quit.

> Being defeated is often a temporary condition. Giving up is what makes it permanent. (Marilyn vos Savant)

Persevering in the face of adversity builds character. Yet most people quit a challenge too easily, too quickly. Joan Chittester says "We quit when we get tired, we quit when others tell us we will never make it, and we quit when we don't see signs of improvement".

Quitting early cements failure. Success follows the creed "I'll just try one more time." A significant problem in education is that children are often protected and deprived of the opportunity to experience setbacks, and consequently do not develop the character required to overcome them.

Perseverance is about finishing tasks and is critical for long-term achievement. In Grit, Angela Duckworth says: "Talent doesn't foster perseverance. Our data show very clearly that there are many talented individuals who simply do not follow through on their commitments. In fact, in our data, grit is usually unrelated or even inversely related to measures of talent". What does encourage perseverance is having a growth mindset.

> Weakness of attitude becomes weakness of character.
> (Einstein)

7 METACOGNITION

> To remain a pupil is to serve your teacher badly.
> (Nietzsche)

The ultimate objective for teachers is to gradually become redundant in the learning lives of their students. Metacognition is that wonderful learning stage when the learner takes responsibility for the learning. An umbrella term, metacognition means "thinking about our thinking". It includes planning, questioning, monitoring, memorisation, self-reflection, self-knowledge about our learning strengths and weaknesses, and self-evaluation. It involves understanding our motivations, setting goals, knowing which practice strategies to implement, and being able to exercise self-discipline. It's about knowing when and how to use these strategies for maximum learning.

In contrast, the skills of super learners are underpinned by executive-function skills and character traits such as sustaining focus, commitment, perseverance, and resisting impulse and distraction.

> I don't divide the world into the weak and the strong, or the successes and the failures. I divide the world into the learners and non-learners. (Benjamin R Barber)

Metacognition is the learner's coming of age. It is the hallmark of intrinsic motivation. The diverse set of skills this word represents is essential for reaching expertise in any domain. This is an important distinction. It's not talent but the processes of development that lead to expertise. But don't expect children to welcome this style of learning. As most teachers find, students actively resist it because it is difficult and requires more mental effort. It's a lot easier to be told what to do and to be evaluated by someone else than to engage with the messiness of learning. Besides, many children have been led to believe it is more important to have the right answers than to ask good questions, or to demonstrate logical learning processes.

Great learning asks great questions, underpinned by great thinking. The brain is more receptive to remember answers to questions we ask than when information is delivered by another. Over time, students should be asking themselves the same questions a teacher would.

The classic sign of passive learning is if the teacher is doing more work than the student, which unfortunately is the norm in many classrooms. Generally, schools fail to teach metacognition; it remains the untaught component of learning. Schools focus more on the transmission of knowledge rather than the transformation of knowledge. It is a travesty that metacognition, the most essential learning-capacity skill set, is overlooked, or at least insufficiently taught. Harvard's David Perkins posits that any substantial improvement in the learning capacity of society is unlikely until metacognitive learning is more fully addressed.

Metacognitive learners take responsibility for their learning. Students must be able to ask, "How effective is my effort? How effective is my learning? What do I need to do to get better? What learning strategy does this task require?" Successful analysis of problems gets to the heart of the matter quickly. Metacognition is not about factual knowledge or skill but the process involved in gaining that knowledge or skill. It enables us to question our beliefs and perspectives that colour our approach and attitude to learning.

Children aged eleven or twelve might have an impressive body of factual knowledge, but have comparatively low metacognitive skills. Metacognition usually flowers later in cognitive development, perhaps in adolescence or early adulthood, but this process is dependent on the quality of teaching and parenting. Young students should be prompted with questions, and encouraged to verbalise thoughts and to self-evaluate.

Midway through my undergraduate education degree I changed piano teachers. My first impression of my new teacher Stephen was that he was a little odd. Stephen barely said a word, so how was I supposed to learn from him? When I played, rather than comment, he looked at me expectantly, as if he were waiting for *me* to do the analysis. Uncomfortable with the silence, I uttered thoughts of my own. "Maybe this phrase could be played softer?" I'd suggest. "OK," he'd say. "Try it." I did so, and the process would be repeated. I might not have understood this at the time but Stephen was teaching me to think for myself, which led me into a new age of self-directed learning. I was learning how to teach myself. Prior to Stephen, my experience with piano lessons was quite different. My role was a passive receiver of teacher knowledge. My well-intentioned teachers always had given me directions and told me what I needed to do, and my job was to sit, listen, obey, and execute. Essentially, this teacher-directed style took the hard work out of learning.

> Let me show you how to do this.
> Let me tell you what you are doing wrong.
> Let me tell you what I think.
> Let me tell you what to do.

This suited me fine because I did not have to think much. But Stephen would have none of this. Great teachers seldom give direct answers or immediate feedback before probing for deeper thought. Teachers who provide solutions before the student has had an opportunity to solve a problem waste a learning opportunity. Rather, good teachers hint, gradually increasing the content until the pupil works it out for themselves. In my example above, as I became more engaged in my own learning, my motivation levels skyrocketed. This was probably my most valuable learning experience as a young adult, and I will always be thankful to Stephen for that.

Questioning

> Never stop questioning. (Einstein)

The simplest strategy for developing metacognition in a child is to ask questions, and allow plenty of time for a response. Simple, open-ended questions prompt self-discovery. Here are some examples.

- How do you think you did?

- Is what you're doing working? Why? Why not?

- Which goals would you like to set for this week?

- What can you do to learn this more thoroughly?

- Can you explain what you are doing? What are you thinking?

- What have you improved upon since last week?

- Can you teach me how to do this?

One study found that over 90 percent of the utterances of the best teachers are questions. Questions are leading and informative, demanding thinking and exploration of ideas. But not all questions are equal. John Hattie's research finds that 60 percent of the 300-400 teacher questions per day require only superficial factual data, 20 percent target procedural knowledge, and only 20 percent are open, skilled questions that prompt deeper thinking and higher-order understanding. When children respond to questions, adults must wait patiently and allow them to struggle to find the right words, resisting the temptation to put words into their mouths. Children need time to process and internalise information before giving a response. This period of silence between a question and response is referred to as "think time". Early studies found that in typical classrooms think time lasted more than 1.5 seconds. By extending this uninterrupted period of silence to just a few more seconds, the length and correctness of responses improves, the number of "I don't know" responses decrease, more students volunteer answers, and overall academic results improve.

Struggle is inherent in learning. This is the principle failing of the enthusiastic graduate teacher, so keen to impart as much as possible of their own knowledge that there is little real learning left for the student to do. Teaching and giving answers are not synonymous. Nor is learning and having the answers supplied. Studies confirm that when teacher talk dominates the learning environment, at best shallow learning results. What teachers choose *not* to say is essential. The best teachers tell their students almost nothing. They prompt and probe, drawing as much as possible from the student. Worse still, teachers who solve problems for students implicitly communicate to the student that they are incapable of solving it for themselves.

> I cannot teach anyone anything, I can only hope to make them think. (Socrates.)

The Socratic method is a questioning pedagogy. A student of Socrates, Plato tells the story of Socrates teaching geometry to a slave boy. Rather than imparting his own knowledge, Socrates uses question alone, thereby allowing the boy to create his own learning. Aldous Huxley was acutely aware of this when he wrote *The Dangers of Good Teaching* in 1927:

> Working on the old-fashioned system, the clever teacher (deplorable paradox!) does almost more harm than the stupid one. For the clever schoolmaster makes things too easy for his pupils; he relieves them of the necessity of finding out things for themselves. By dint of brilliant teaching he succeeds in almost eliminating the learning process. He knows how to fill his pupils with ready-made knowledge,

which they inevitably forget (since it is not their knowledge and cost them nothing to acquire), as soon as the examination for which it was required is safely passed.

The stupid teacher, on the other hand, may be so completely intolerable that the child will perhaps be driven, despairingly and in mere self-defence, to educate himself; in which case the incompetent shepherd will have done, all unwittingly, a great service to his charge, by forcing him into a rebellious intellectual independence.

Initially, mastering a skill is procedural. That is, children know how to do things but cannot explain the process using words. A deeper knowing, declarative knowledge is the ability to talk and think about learning using linguistic terms. Allowing students to talk about concepts in their own words strengthens understanding from the procedural realm to include the declarative realm. Words enhance conceptual understanding; they enable us to think. Complex thoughts are not possible without them.

Self-Talk (Verbal Mediation)

> Of course I talk to myself; sometimes I need expert advice!
> (Thomas Jefferson)

Abraham Lincoln's secretary asked him, "Sir, why do you read aloud to yourself, and why do you talk to yourself?" Lincoln's response was, "When I do this, I remember twice as much, for twice as long".

This is self-talk, another strategy for increasing metacognition.

Self-talk, or verbal mediation, is thinking aloud. When children encounter a learning difficulty, ask them to think verbally. By thinking out loud they are more likely to uncover the root of a problem and gain a better understanding of the task. Also, we gain insight into children's mental processes. More generally, reading aloud helps us process information in the mind, and helps us to stay in the present. Steven Mithen writes "Children who provide their own verbal commentary learn skills quicker than those who remain silent". Self-talk is essential for a child's development and, although it gradually disappears as thinking becomes silent, we continue to do it occasionally – particularly if faced with a challenging problem. Verbal cues assist with thinking, memory formation, focus, and learning in general. For example, memorising a list of words by saying them out loud is more effective than through silent reading.

Reflection

> Learning without thought is labour lost. Thought without learning is perilous. (Confucius)

Metacognition is reflective. Confucius said activity and reflection must complement and support each other. Action by itself is blind, but reflection alone is impotent. More broadly, Confucius continued, evil is bolstered by the lack of self-reflection, self-awareness, and self-knowledge. Metacognition encourages us to look within. Making time for reflection before and after a learning activity is important. Teenage boys lag girls in reflective skills. They tend to overestimate their capabilities and underestimate the time it takes to learn. Parents create opportunities for reflection by asking questions. Explicit reflection helps children to become intrinsically motivated and independent learners.

> Man's release from tutelage is enlightenment. His tutelage is his inability to make use of his understanding without guidance from another. (Immanuel Kant)

Metacognition provides us with this objective view of why we do what we do. It enables freedom of the mind. Through reflection and evaluation, we understand our actions more critically.

> We cannot come fully to life without it [metacognition]. The alternative is to consume someone else's thoughts by copying the opinions of another, repeat the ideas of others, critique nothing. We become clones of those around us.
> (Joan Chittester)

Above are three strategies for developing metacognition in children: questioning, verbalisation, and reflection. But the most effective way to gain insights into the learning process is to teach someone else. Teaching is a dynamic mix of reflection, questioning, and explaining. It wins the gold medal in the metacognition stakes. "Can you teach me how to do this?"

8   IQ AND INTELLIGENCE

French psychologist Alfred Binet was sure that if he could identify children with serious learning difficulties he could address these through early intervention. Originally developed in 1904 and revised in 1916, Binet's concept of the intelligence quotient (IQ) became the premier calculating tool for general intelligence. An advocate of the growth intelligence mindset, Binet believed people could increase their intelligence through intellectual effort and exercise. Binet, however, feared that his theory could be taken out of context. "A few modern philosophers…assert that an individual's intelligence is a fixed quantity, a quantity which cannot be increased," Binet wrote in 1911. "We must protest and react against this brutal pessimism…. With practice, training, and above all, method, we manage to increase our attention, our memory, our judgment and literally become more intelligent than we were before".[33]

Binet's fears were well founded for at that time the English psychologist Charles Spearman was putting forward a theory which argued that intelligence is general, singular, and fixed. Spearman's ideas spread, and his concept of intelligence has been widely accepted ever since.

IQ testing is prevalent today. It measures linguistic and analytical skills, spatial orientation, and logical reasoning. It does not measure abilities necessary for art, music, creativity and innovation, dance and

---

[33] Binet, A. 1984. Modern Ideas About Children. Menlo Park: Suzanne Heisler. First published in French in 1911.

athletic ability, the ability to get along with other people, or self-knowledge. However, when children learn new skills, the rate of initial learning does correlate with IQ because of the ability of higher-IQ children to remember rules and follow directions. But it would be a mistake to select these children for special attention, because this does not mean that the initial IQ advantages persist for the longer term. Anders Ericsson explains in *Peak:*

> As they develop in competence we see little or no relationship between IQ and expertise. Those with lower IQs tend to engage in more practice – because they don't find it so *easy* in the first place, and thereby surpass higher IQ students. It would be a mistake to select for long-term potential based on IQ. The IQ advantage gets smaller over time, with the quality and quantity of practice taking over (as the major determinant in the development of skill). This is why it is so difficult to predict who will reach the top in any given field. No one has ever figured out how to identify people with innate talent.

Numerous studies have found only a low correlation between IQ and the achievement of goals. Daniel Goleman claims that IQ accounts for only 4 to 6 percent of life achievement, while Harvard University's Howard Gardner figures that IQ predicts approximately 6 to 10 percent of career accomplishment.

Numeracy + Literacy = INTELLIGENCE

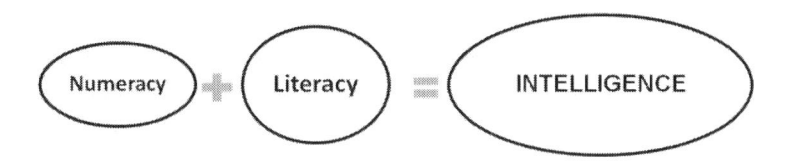

Most school education is IQ-centric and places pronounced emphasis on the disciplines of mathematics, science, and literacy. Whilst important, this does not represent the full value and richness of human intelligence. Ask any student what it means to be smart, and the response almost certainly will be bound to literacy and numeracy. Children value what is tested, and numeracy and literacy are the most frequently tested skills in schools. Literacy, and to a lesser extent numeracy, are essential living skills, but there are other ways of knowing and understanding that deserve integral places in education.

Higher IQ has been related to a healthier life, longer life expectancy and greater earning potential, but the model lacks broadness and inclusivity. It is congruent with fixed intelligence because in IQ theory test scores do not significantly change over time. IQ theory limits human potential. It fails to acknowledge that when we exercise the brain, we increase our intellectual potential.

For many years, the IQ model of intelligence has been responsible for pushing people away from learning. If you were not successful at numeracy or literacy, you were labelled as dumb, or stupid. This intellectual scar has led to a high proportion of adults doubting their ability to learn new things, and discourages them from engaging in the joys of lifelong learning. Children who adopt a fixed view of intelligence tend to work less hard than others and are more likely to prematurely give up on a task. As explained earlier, attributions such as "I'm just not good at this" reveal deterministic and fixed beliefs about learning potential. A lack of belief in one's present ability, or one's potential, results in poor self-esteem. Poor self-esteem not only is unhealthy for the individual, but also results in all manner of community problems.

> The greatest evil that can befall man is that he should come to think ill of himself. (Goethe)

Multiple Intelligence

> All cultures deserve a seat at the council of human knowledge. (Edmund Wade Davis)

Individuals who excel in numeracy and literacy are labelled "intelligent", whilst those of sport, musical and other artistic ability are "talented". The latter proposes a genetic endowment. In his 1983 book *Frames of Mind: The Theory of Multiple Intelligences,* Howard Gardner broadened the narrow IQ intelligence model into a multidimensional one.

Gardner's redefinition of intelligence encourages a pursuit of personal interests. There are many ways of expressing intelligence, not just two. Thankfully, the mysteries of curiosity ensure humanity's rich functional and cultural diversity. We are offered this extraordinary opportunity; with training and effort, we can improve at anything. Some pursue singular expertise, others become a jack of all trades. Many of us like to become excellent at one endeavour, and maintain a healthy level of proficiency with other interests. The basic purpose of education is to broaden the potential of human intelligence and enjoyment of life.

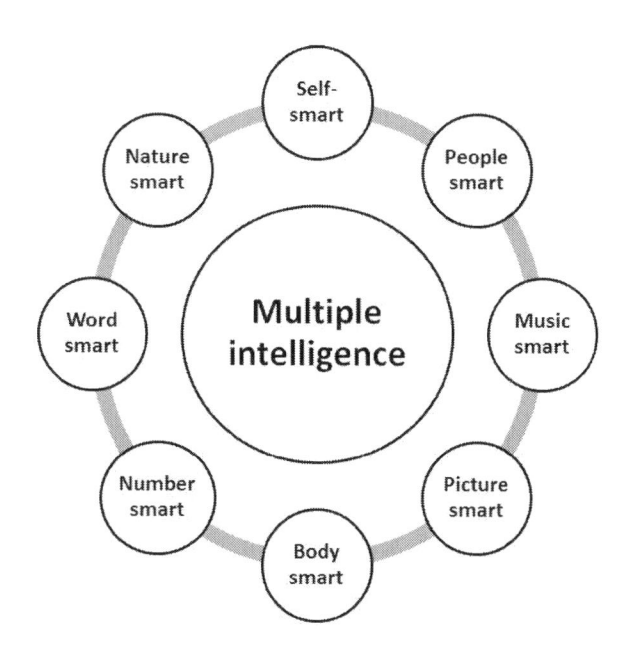

```
                    Self-
                    smart
        Nature                  People
        smart                   smart

        Word        Multiple    Music
        smart       intelligence smart

        Number                  Picture
        smart                   smart
                    Body
                    smart
```

Know something about everything and everything about something. (T. Huxley)

Life is interdisciplinary and multisensory. We learn through the senses and embrace the richness of multi-discipline opportunity and experience. The richer the sensory diet, the more complex the brain becomes. For example, material presented with pictures and sound makes information easier to remember and more enjoyable to learn. The most effective memory-building techniques are based on the principle of association, and the strongest associations are sensory and emotional. This is the essence of multisensory learning.

> Our senses evolved to work together…which means that we learn best if we stimulate several senses at once. (John Medina)

Subject compartmentalisation results in curricula that lack context and are reductionist and fragmented. Interdisciplinary education is an approach that makes connections between subjects. Finding connections between disparate bodies of knowledge stimulates creative possibility, and fostering creativity is an overarching aim in just about every curriculum statement worldwide.

> A real education is the ability to perceive hidden connections between phenomena. (Václav Havel)

> What's in greatest demand today is not analysis but synthesis—seeing the big picture, crossing boundaries, and being able to combine disparate pieces into an arresting new whole. (Daniel Pink)

Many of the world's foremost thinkers synthesised ideas across subject areas. Pythagoras of Ancient Greece (570–490 BC) believed that by connecting the properties of different doctrines he could discover the secrets of the world. Pythagoras was fascinated by the relationships between music, numbers, the cosmos, and psychology.

Possibly the greatest multi-intelligent person was Leonardo da Vinci. This list hardly does him justice, but his occupations included painter, musician, inventor, scientist, sculptor, architect, mathematician, and writer. Da Vinci's approach to learning was cognitive and sensory. He studied the art of science and the science of art. Like Pythagoras, da Vinci believed that every part of the universe is linked and thus affects every other part. More recently, former Australian Prime Minister Paul Keating said that rationalism without a higher and more conceptual "poetic strand of life" is incomplete. Keating discusses the power of synthesis, between beauty and reason, in his 2011 book *After Words*. His inspiration comes from music and beauty. Keating says:

> Music has always been a large part of what makes me tick. When I was listening to music I would always have the pad out to write the ideas down. You listen to a great work, something that was created afresh; you hear the majesty of these works and your head and soul get caught up in them. When that happens, you are in for bigger things and you will strike out to be better.[34]

For a flourishing society, specialists are important, but not sufficient. We also need synthesists and big-picture thinkers. Creativity expert Hideaki Koizumi says "Great innovation and new ideas emerge from trans-disciplinary connections".

---

[34] Paul Kelly, Oct. 22, 2012. The Australian.

9   CREATIVITY

> There is nothing more marvellous than thinking of a new idea.
>
> There is nothing more magnificent than seeing a new idea working.
>
> There is nothing more useful than a new idea that serves your purpose. (Edward de Bono)

A 2010 IBM survey of more than 1,500 CEOs from 60 countries found that the most crucial factor for future success is creativity.

In broader terms, free imaginative play is crucial for social, emotional and cognitive development. "Just playing" is what education experts consider the best way for young children to learn about peer relationships, and is important for academic success later in life. Free play refers to unstructured play in that the activity need not have an obvious function or a clear goal. Games might be fun ways to learn socially, emotionally and cognitively, but free play is different. Unlike games that have an existing set of rules that someone else created, free play has no rules and thereby generates more creative possibilities and responses. This challenges the brain more than following predetermined rules because children are required to use their imagination and to try out new ideas. Recent evidence suggests that a lack of opportunity for unstructured and imaginative free play in childhood can affect children's later social development, behavioural flexibility, ability to cope with stress, and development of problem-solving skills. Since the early 1980s, a trend has arisen in which children's free playtime is diminishing. Parents may underestimate the value of free play in favour of more structured activities that are assumed to deliver more valuable learning outcomes.

> Time is a game played beautifully by children.
> (Heraclitus)

Students who learn in creative ways learn well. Creative learning is fun, engaging, and motivating. It requires identifying problems, considering multiple possibilities, making decisions, and finding solutions. Creative people are more likely to have a growth-intelligence mindset. They are open to new experiences, prepared to take risks, to make mistakes, and to fail. They allow their imaginations to be inspired by anything and everything, including the sounds around them, nature, art, and music. They have heroes and role models, and delight in examples of excellence. While an individual cannot be creative without acting intelligently, creative people are not necessarily the smartest in their domain. In the confines of the old IQ system there is a correlation linking creativity with intelligence only up to the threshold score of approximately 120. This implies that creative people need to be reasonably intelligent, but not excessively so.

Twelve Suggestions for Fostering Creativity

1. The most limited resource in education is time. Playing with ideas takes time. Allocate sufficient time to experiment with

ideas. Jean-Jacques Rousseau said, "The most useful rule of education is not to save time, but to lose it". Creative learning requires personal space.

2. Copy! Explore other people's work and their way of doing things. Many great works of art began with inspiration from the work of others. Copying is a natural way to learn, and the best way to investigate greatness.

> I don't improvise anything original, as far as I know. I think it's all pieces of stuff that I've heard throughout the years. (Bob Stoloff)

3. Maximise opportunities for choice, tempered with an understanding that too much choice can be overwhelming. Allow children the freedom to approach an activity *their* way. Autonomy is at the heart of intrinsic motivation and gives students a sense of ownership. Provide opportunities for self-initiated learning in an environment that avoids overly detailed supervision. The conditions are now ripe for children's natural curiosity, the precursor of an intrinsic love of learning, to flourish.

4. Creativity involves asking great questions. Encourage lots of questions and tease them out for children to solve. Adults can be in too much of a hurry to satisfy a child's curiosity. Rather than providing answers for them, allow more *wait* time for them to find their own answers.

> Let him sit with the problem for a while and solve it himself. Let him know nothing because you have told him, but because he has learnt it for himself. Let the children discover. (Jean-Jacques Rousseau)

That lover of wisdom Confucius said that he would not teach anyone who "has not been driven crazy trying to understand a problem". Allowing questions to remain unanswered for a while will arouse intense curiosity. This can be exploited and even contrived by presenting incomplete or contradictory information about a topic. It is this lack of completeness that compels one to understand it further.

> Wonder is the seed of knowledge. (Francis Bacon)

5. Allow children to challenge key assumptions and break rules. In schools, much of education is convergent in that student work heads towards a singular pre-existing answer. Don't fall into the science trap. Students rarely conduct experiments in science classes; they undertake contrived demonstrations designed to converge with an expected and known outcome. Creativity is about exploring possibilities and choosing from a range of solutions.
6. Encourage and engage children with the concept of idea improvement. Edward de Bono says, "Most people look for creative solutions when things are not going well, but continuous improvement even when things are going well is

an area ripe for creative thinking". Complacency and self-satisfaction are the enemy of creative improvement.

Creativity is seeing what everyone else has seen, and thinking what no one else has thought. (Einstein)

7. Use the word *imagine*. Imagination is the capacity to think in terms of possibility, an essential ingredient for creative outcomes. Children will see many possibilities that adults may not.

Never stop imagining. Imagination is greater than knowledge. (Einstein)

8. Inspire students through personal, historical, and peer examples. Heroes open our eyes, redefining the boundaries of possibility. Children need opportunities to collaborate on projects with others. Real learning occurs when like-minded people share ideas.

9. Draw connections between the various multiple intelligence strands. All things in the universe are related, and new patterns and understandings continually emerge. Creative people find relationships the rest of us never notice. The broader and richer the experiences the greater the tools for creativity. To generate creative thoughts, get walking. A 2014 study from Stanford University found that when walking rather than sitting people were 60 percent more creative. Beethoven's favorite evening activity was a two-hour walk, carrying with

him writing materials to capture any inspired ideas. On the other hand, walking is not good for convergent thinking such as computation. Compute 46 x 23 as you walk and you will probably find you need to stop or at least slow down. As Daniel Kahneman says, "intense concentration requires stillness".[35]

Exercise can turn you into a sharper version of yourself.
(John Medina)

10. For creative tasks, formative feedback is more important than evaluation. Grades and quantitative measures, labelling, and tracking undermine intrinsic motivation and can shut down creative effort. Rather than offering rewards, adults should encourage children to appreciate and be pleased with their own creative efforts. Instead of comparing their creative work with others, have children reflect verbally on their own work. Adults must be mindful of their own preoccupation with judgement and comparison.

11. Encourage risk taking in a non-threatening atmosphere for relaxed and enjoyable learning. Fear of mistakes or failure stifles creative effort because innovation requires experimentation, which implies uncertain outcomes. Creative people make mistakes more often than non-creative people because they see mistakes as necessary for learning.

---

[35] Kahneman, D. 2011. Thinking, Fast and Slow. New York: Farrar, Straus and Giroux.

> Success is going from failure to failure without losing enthusiasm. (Winston Churchill)
>
> Creativity is allowing yourself to make mistakes. Art is knowing which ones to keep. (Scott Adams)

12. Allow children to connect with people who are different. Alternative points of view challenge one's thinking, causing a re-examination of ideas. This can catalyse creativity and innovation.

Creativity does not mean anything goes. Bizarre is not necessarily creative. Creativity is more about an appropriate, purposeful, but unexpected response. It requires discipline and making deliberate and informed choices. Creative people know *why* they do *what* they do. Creativity does not need to be complex or profound. The classic appeal for many of the world's greatest art works is beauty and simplicity.

> A theory is the more impressive the greater is the simplicity of its premises, the more different are the kinds of things it relates and the more extended the range of its applicability. (Einstein)

BIBLIOGRAPHY

Berger, R. 2003. An Ethic of Excellence. Portsmouth: Heinemann.

Cisksentmihalyi, M. 1990. Flow: The Psychology of Optimal Experience. Colvin,

G. 2008. Talent is Overrated: What Really Separates World-class Performers from Everybody Else. London: Nicholas Brealey.

Coyle, D. 2009. The Talent Code. New York: Bantam Books.

New York: Harper Perennial.

De Bono, E. 1995. Serious Creativity. New York: HarperCollins.

Dweck, C. 2008. Mindset: The New Psychology of Success. USA: Ballantine Books Inc.

Gladwell, M. 2008. Outliers. London: Penguin.

Goleman, D. 1997. Emotional Intelligence: Why It Can Matter More Than IQ. New York: Bantam Books.

Griffin, M. 2013 Learning Strategies for Musical Success. Adelaide. Music Education World.

Howe, M. J. 1999. Genius Explained. Cambridge: Cambridge University Press.

Howe, M. J. A., Davidson, J. W., Moore, D. G. & Sloboda, J. A. 1998. Innate talents: Reality or myth? Behavioural and Brain Sciences. 21, 399–442.

Kahneman, D. 2011. Thinking, fast and slow. New York: Farrar, Straus and Giroux.

Lang L. 2008. Journey of a Thousand Miles. Spiegel & Grau.

Levitin, D. 2006. This Is Your Brain on Music: The Science of a Human

McGilchrist, I. 2009. The Master and his Emissary: The Divided Brain and the Making of the Western World. New Haven. Yale University Press.

McPherson, G. E. and McCormick, J. 1999. Motivational and Self-Regulated Learning Components of Musical Practice. Bulletin of the Council for Research in Music Education 141:98.

Medina, J. 2015. Brain Rules. Seattle: Pear Press.

Mithen, S. 2005. The Singing Neanderthals. London: Weidenfeld & Nicolson.

Neff, K. 2011. Self-Compassion, London: Hodder & Stoughton.

Rainey, L.D. 2010. Confucius & Confucianism The Essentials. Malden, Mass:

Wiley-Blackwell.

Sternberg, R, J & Grigorenko, E. L. Teaching for Successful Intelligence to Increase Student learning and Achievement. Arlington Heights: Skylight.

Werner, K. 1996 Effortless Mastery, USA: Jamey Aebersold.

ABOUT THE AUTHOR

Michael Griffin is an educator, speaker, author, conductor and pianist. Michael's talks are inspired by theory of motivation and the premise that the greatest predictor of progress is the quality and the quantity of effort. He has spoken to groups of staff, students, parents and community audiences in more than 300 schools and conferences in 25 countries around the world. Michael has been the Keynote or Consultant Speaker at several global education events including the European Council for International Schools (Hamburg and Nice), Association of International Schools Africa Educators' Conference (South Africa), English Schools' Foundation (Hong Kong), International Educators Conference (Brunei), APEP Member Schools Conference (Thailand), British Schools of the Middle East Arts Conference (Oman and Dubai), Spring Cantus Salisburgensis Festival (Austria), Hampshire Music Service (UK), Association Genevoise des Ecoles Privées (Switzerland), and numerous local conferences throughout Australia. He has consulted for Cambridge University Press designing curriculum for Kazakhstan. As a conductor, Michael's choral ensembles have received more than 40 prizes and awards in Australian competitions including Australia's major choral prize, the Australasian Open Choral Championship. As a pianist, he has held guest residencies at Dubai's Burj al Arab and Australia's Hayman Island. Classical piano recordings include the compilations Consolation (2013) and Shimmer (2014). As a teacher in schools, Michael has held a range of posts up to Deputy Head level. Michael is a recipient of the South Australian Education and Arts Ministers' Prize, and is listed in the inaugural Who's Who South Australia for services to education.

Printed in Great Britain
by Amazon

www.theflutetutor.co.uk
Tel. 07766 467261

CHILDREN & LEARNING

for Parents

Michael Griffin

Published by Music Education World

Adelaide, Australia

First Published 2017

Copyright © 2017 Michael Griffin

All rights reserved.